AMERICA

RECONSTRUCTION
1865—1890

Ulysses S. Grant

AMERICA

Great Crises In Our History
Told by Its Makers

A LIBRARY OF ORIGINAL SOURCES

Volume IX
Reconstruction
1865—1890

ISSUED BY

AMERICANIZATION DEPARTMENT

VETERANS OF FOREIGN WARS
OF THE
UNITED STATES

CHICAGO, U. S. A.

Copyright 1925
Americanization Department
Veterans of Foreign Wars
of the United States

TABLE OF CONTENTS

VOLUME IX

	PAGE
ROBERT E. LEE'S ATTITUDE AFTER THE WAR. His Own Written Statement	13
GENERAL GRANT REVIEWS POST-WAR CONDITIONS IN THE SOUTH. His Report to President Johnson	16
LAYING THE FIRST SUCCESSFUL ATLANTIC CABLE. By Cyrus W. Field	20
WHY THE UNITED STATES WANTED ALASKA. By Senator Charles Sumner	31
THE PURCHASE OF ALASKA. By Frederic Bancroft	38
HUNTING BUFFALO TO FEED THE RAILROAD BUILDERS. By William F. (Buffalo Bill) Cody	43
THE THREATENED IMPEACHMENT OF ANDREW JOHNSON. By Senator Shelby M. Cullom	48
THE FOURTEENTH AMENDMENT. By Representative Thaddeus Stevens	63
ULYSSES S. GRANT, EIGHTEENTH PRESIDENT. By James Ford Rhodes	69
BLACK FRIDAY. By J. K. Medbery	76
THE FIRST TRANSCONTINENTAL RAILROAD. By John P. Davis	87
THE OVERTHROW OF THE TWEED RING. By E. Benjamin Andrews	97

TABLE OF CONTENTS

	PAGE
THE FIFTEENTH AMENDMENT. By Senator Henry Wilson	105
THE KU-KLUX KLAN. By the Federal Grand Jury	110
THE GENEVA AWARD IN THE ALABAMA CLAIMS. By the Arbitrators	115
THE GREAT CHICAGO FIRE. By Horace White	126
THE GREELEY CAMPAIGN. By James G. Blaine	143
CARPET-BAG GOVERNMENT. By James Shepherd Pike	152
THE PANIC OF 1873. By E. Benjamin Andrews	159
CUBAN INTERVENTION PROPOSED. By Hamilton Fish, Secretary of State	167
THE CENTENNIAL OF THE REPUBLIC. A Contemporary Account	175
THE HAYES-TILDEN PRESIDENTIAL CONTEST. By Edward Stanwood	185
CUSTER'S LAST STAND. By Judson Elliott Walker	195
THE COMING OF THE TELEPHONE. By Thomas A. Watson	207
UNCLE SAM RESUMES SPECIE PAYMENTS. By Secretary of the Treasury John Sherman	221
EDISON'S ELECTRIC LIGHT INVENTION. By Frank L. Dyar and Thomas C. Martin	226
CIVIL SERVICE REFORM DEMANDED. By George William Curtis	231
NORTH AMERICAN RELATIONS TO SOUTH AMERICA. By James G. Blaine, Secretary of State	237
THE ASSASSINATION OF GARFIELD. By Theodore Clarke Smith	242

TABLE OF CONTENTS

PAGE

THE BLAINE-CLEVELAND CAMPAIGN. By Harry Thurston Peck 251

THE DEATH AND FUNERAL OF GENERAL GRANT. By General James Grant Wilson 266

THE CHICAGO HAYMARKET RIOT. By Harry Thurston Peck 274

THE INTERSTATE COMMERCE COMMISSION. By Aldace Freeman Walker 282

THE PRESIDENTIAL CAMPAIGN OF 1888. By Edward Stanwood 287

DISPUTING THE SAMOAN ISLANDS WITH GERMANY. By Harry Thurston Peck 293

THE MCKINLEY TARIFF BILL. By Charles Sumner Olcott 304

BEHRING SEA TROUBLES WITH GREAT BRITAIN. From Official Documents 309

RECONSTRUCTION
1865—1890

ROBERT E. LEE'S ATTITUDE AFTER THE WAR

His Own Written Statement

LEE, to whom Lincoln had first offered the command of the United States Army, in April, 1861, and had declined it, stating that, "though opposed to secession and deprecating war," he "could take no part in the invasion of the Southern States," ranks as the greatest of the Confederate leaders, not only because of his military genius, but for the magnanimous way in which he accepted the result. This letter, addressed to a personal friend, in September, 1865, is valued as an important document in evidence of his desire to infuse others with his own spirit. It is taken from the Rev. J. W. Jones's "Personal Recollections of Lee," published in 1875.

A month after writing this letter, General Lee was installed as president of Washington College at Lexington, Virginia, now Washington and Lee University—a post which he held until his death, October 12, 1870.

I HAVE received your letter of the 23d ult. [August, 1865], and in reply will state the course I have pursued under circumstances similar to your own, and will leave you to judge of its propriety. Like yourself, I have, since the cessation of hostilities, advised all with whom I have conversed on the subject, who come within the terms of the President's proclamations, to take the oath of allegiance, and accept in good faith the amnesty offered.

But I have gone further, and have recommended to those who were excluded from their benefits to make application under the proviso of the proclamation of the 29th of May, to be embraced in its provisions. Both classes, in order to be restored to their former rights and privileges, were required to perform a certain act, and I do not see that an acknowledgment of fault is expressed in one more than the other. The war being at an end, the Southern States have laid down their arms, and the question at issue between them and the Northern States having been decided, I believe it to be the duty of every one to unite in the restoration of the country, and the reëstablishment of peace and harmony.

These considerations governed me in the counsels I gave to others, and induced me on the 13th of June to make application to be included in the terms of the amnesty proclamation. I have not received an answer, and cannot inform you what has been the decision of the President. But, whatever that may be, I do not see how the course I have recommended and practiced can prove detrimental to the former President of the Confederate States.

It appears to me that the allayment of passion, the dissipation of prejudice, and the restoration of reason, will alone enable the people of the country to acquire a true knowledge and form a correct judgment of the events of the past four years. It will, I think, be admitted that Mr. Davis has done nothing more than all the citizens of the Southern States, and should not be held accountable for acts performed by them in the exercise of what had been considered by them unquestionable right. I have too exalted an opinion of the American people to believe that they will consent to injustice; and it is only necessary, in my opinion, that truth should be known, for the rights of every one to be secured. I know of no surer way of eliciting the truth than by burying contention with the war.

GENERAL GRANT REVIEWS POST-WAR CONDITIONS IN THE SOUTH

His Report to President Johnson

ANDREW JOHNSON, a North Carolinian, who had risen from the position of a tailor to the Vice-Presidency, succeeded to the Presidency on the death of Lincoln. As President he reversed his attitude toward the South, and soon proclaimed a general policy of leniency toward the seceded States. As a step in that direction, he requested Grant, for whom Congress had created the full rank of General, to tour the South and prepare for him (Johnson) the accompanying report of conditions as he found them.

Throughout this trying period Grant maintained a loyal and dignified position, but was drawn into the struggle between the President and Congress as it became intensified. He was inclined to support Johnson, who characterized the course of Congress toward the South as another rebellion. It was while Grant was on this mission that the Wade-Davis Reconstruction Bill, aimed as a gun at Johnson, was passed by a defiant Congress.

WITH your approval, and also that of the honorable Secretary of War, I left Washington City on the 27th of last month (November) for the purpose of making a tour of inspection through some of the Southern States, or States lately in rebellion, and to see what changes were necessary to be made in the disposition of the military forces of the country; how these forces could be reduced and expenses curtailed, etc.; and to learn, as far as possible, the feelings and intentions of the citizens of those States toward the general Government. The following are the conclusions come to by me:

I am satisfied that the mass of thinking men of the South accept the present situation of affairs in good faith. The questions which have heretofore divided the sentiment of the people of the two sections—slavery and State rights, or the right of a State to secede from the Union—they regard as having been settled forever by the highest tribunal—arms—that man can resort to. I was pleased to learn from the leading men whom I met that they not only accepted the decision arrived at as final, but, now that the smoke of battle has cleared away, and time has been given for reflection, that this decision has been a fortunate one for the whole country, they receiving like benefits from it with those who opposed them in the field and in council.

Four years of war, during which law was executed only at the point of the bayonet throughout the States in rebellion, have left the people possibly in a condition not to yield that ready obedience to civil authority the American people have generally been in the habit of yielding. This would render the presence of small garrisons throughout those States necessary until such time as labor returns to its proper channel, and civil authority is fully established. I did not meet any one, either those holding places under the Government or citizens of the Southern States, who think it practicable to withdraw the military from the South at present. The white and the black mutually require the protection of the general government.

There is such universal acquiescence in the authority of the general government throughout the portions of country visited by me, that the mere presence of a military force, without regard to numbers, is sufficient to maintain order. The good of the country, and economy, require that the force is kept in the interior, where there are many freedmen (elsewhere in the Southern States than at forts upon the sea coast no force is necessary), should all be white troops. The reasons for this are obvious without mentioning many of them. The presence of black troops, lately slaves, demoralizes labor, both by their advice and by furnishing in their camps a resort for the freedmen for long distances around. White troops generally excite no opposition, and therefore a small number of them can maintain order in a given district. Colored troops must be kept in bodies sufficient to defend themselves. It is not the thinking men who would use violence toward any class of troops sent among them by the general government, but the ignorant in some places might; and the late slave seems to be imbued with the idea that the property of his late master should, by right, belong to him, or, at least, should have no protection from the colored soldier. There is danger of collisions being brought on by such causes.

My observations lead me to the conclusion that the citizens of the Southern States are anxious to return to self-government, within the Union, as soon as possible; that while reconstructing they want and require protection from the government; that they are in earnest in wishing to do what they think is required by the Government, not humiliating to them as citizens, and that if such a course were pointed out they would pursue it in good faith. It is to be regretted that there cannot be a greater commingling, at this time, between the citizens of the two sections, and particularly of those intrusted with the law-making power.

LAYING THE FIRST SUCCESSFUL ATLANTIC CABLE

By Cyrus W. Field

HENRY M. FIELD, brother of Cyrus W. Field, its chief promoter, has told the story (Volume VII) of the first Atlantic cable laid in 1858. After a few hundred messages were transmitted it ceased to work. In this account, written in 1866, Cyrus Field resumes the wonder-story where it was left off eight years previously, and carries it to the successful establishment of the enterprise, in September, 1866. Since then cable communication between Europe and America has been uninterrupted.

In view of its long and continuous success, it is hard to realize the obstacles Field had to surmount. In the face of disheartening failures he never despaired of the triumph achieved July 27, 1866, when the "Great Eastern" reached Newfoundland without a mishap, and the land connection was made. Other brothers of the promoter were Stephen J. Field, United States Supreme Court Justice, and David Dudley Field, the eminent lawyer.

AFTER the failure of 1858 came our darkest days. When a thing is dead, it is hard to galvanize it into life. It is more difficult to revive an old enterprise than to start a new one. The freshness and novelty are gone, and the feeling of disappointment discourages further effort.

Other causes delayed a new attempt. The United States had become involved in a tremendous war; and while the nation was struggling for life, it had no time to spend in foreign enterprises. But in England the project was still kept alive. The Atlantic Telegraph Company kept up its organization. It had a noble body of directors, who had faith in the enterprise and looked beyond its present low estate to ultimate success. Our chairman, the Right Honorable James Stuart Wortley, did not join us in the hour of victory, but in what seemed the hour of despair, after the failure of 1858, and he has been a steady support through all these years.

All this time the science of submarine telegraphy was making progress. The British Government appointed a commission to investigate the whole subject. It was composed of eminent scientific men and practical engineers—Galton, Wheatstone, Fairbairn, Bidder, Varley and Latimer and Edwin Clark—with the secretary of the company, Mr. Saward—names to be held in honor in connection with this enterprise, along with those of other English engineers, such as Stephenson and Brunel and Whitworth and Penn and Lloyd and Joshua Field, who gave time and thought and labor freely to this enterprise, refusing all compensation. This commission sat for nearly two years, and spent many thousands of pounds in experiments. The result was a clear conviction in every mind that it was possible to lay a telegraph across the Atlantic. Science was also being all the while applied to practice. Submarine cables were laid in different seas—in the Mediterranean, in the Red Sea, and the Persian Gulf. The last was laid by my friend Sir Charles Bright.

When the scientific and engineering problems were solved, we took heart again and began to prepare for a fresh attempt. This was in 1863. In the United States—though the war was still raging—I went from city to city, holding meetings and trying to raise capital, but with poor success. Men came and listened and said it was all very fine and hoped I would succeed, but did nothing. In one of the cities they gave me a large meeting and passed some beautiful resolutions and appointed a committee of "solid men" to canvass the city, but I did not get a solitary subscriber! In New York city I did better, though money came by the hardest effort. By personal solicitations, encouraged by good friends, I succeeded in raising three hundred and fifty thousand dollars. Since not many had faith, I must present one example to the contrary, though it was not till a year later. When almost all deemed it a hopeless scheme, one gentleman came to me and purchased stock of the Atlantic Telegraph Company to the amount of one hundred thousand dollars. That was Mr. Loring Andrews. But at the time I speak of, it was plain that our main hope must be in England, and I went to London. There, too, it dragged heavily. There was a profound discouragement. Many had lost before, and were not willing to throw more money into the sea. We needed six hundred thousand pounds, and with our utmost efforts we had raised less than half, and there the enterprise stood in a deadlock. It was plain that we must have help from some new quarter. I looked around to find a man who had broad shoulders and could carry a heavy load, and who would be a giant in the cause.

LAYING THE FIRST SUCCESSFUL CABLE   23

At this time I was introduced to a gentleman, whom I would hold up to the American public as a specimen of a great-hearted Englishman, Mr. Thomas Brassey. In London he is known as one of the men who have made British enterprise and British capital felt in all parts of the earth. I went to see him, though with fear and trembling. He received me kindly, but put me through such an examination as I never had before. I thought I was in the witness-box. He asked me every possible question, but my answers satisfied him, and he ended by saying it was an enterprise that should be carried out, and that he would be one of ten men to furnish the money to do it. This was a pledge of sixty thousand pounds sterling! Encouraged by this noble offer, I looked around to find another such man, though it was almost like trying to find two Wellingtons. But he was found in Mr. John Pender, of Manchester. I went to his office in London one day, and we walked together to the House of Commons, and before we got there he said he would take an equal share with Mr. Brassey.

The action of these two gentlemen was a turning-point in the history of our enterprise; for it led shortly after to a union of the well-known firm of Glass, Elliott & Company, with the Guttapercha Company, making of the two one concern known as the Telegraph Construction and Maintenance Company, which included not only Mr. Brassey and Mr. Pender, but other men of great wealth, such as Mr. George Elliott, and Mr. Barclay of London, and Mr. Henry

Bewley of Dublin, and which, thus reënforced with immense capital, took up the whole enterprise in its strong arms. We needed, I have said, six hundred thousand pounds, and with all our efforts in England and America we raised only two hundred eighty-five thousand pounds. This new company now came forward, and offered to take the whole remaining three hundred fifteen thousand pounds, besides one hundred thousand pounds of the bonds, and to make its own profits contingent on success. Mr. Richard A. Glass was made managing director and gave energy and vigor to all its departments, being admirably seconded by the secretary, Mr. Shuter.

A few days after, half a dozen gentlemen joined together and bought the "Great Eastern" to lay the cable; and at the head of this company was placed Mr. Daniel Gooch, a member of Parliament, and chairman of the Great Western Railway, who was with us in both the expeditions which followed. His son, Mr. Charles Gooch, a volunteer in the service, worked faithfully on board the "Great Eastern."

The good fortune which favored us in our ship favored us also in our commander, Captain Anderson, who was for years in the Cunard Line. How well he did his part in two expeditions the result has proved, and it was just that a mark of royal favor should fall on that manly head. Thus organized, the work of making a new Atlantic cable was begun. The core was prepared with infinite care, under the able superintendence of Mr. Chatterton and Mr. Willoughby

LAYING THE FIRST SUCCESSFUL CABLE

Smith, and the whole was completed in about eight months. As fast as ready, it was taken on board the "Great Eastern" and coiled in three enormous tanks, and on July 15, 1865, the ship sailed.

I will not stop to tell the story of that expedition. For a week all went well; we had paid out one thousand two hundred miles of cable, and had only six hundred miles farther to go, when, hauling in the cable to remedy a fault, it parted and went to the bottom. That day I never can forget—how men paced the deck in despair, looking out on the broad sea that had swallowed up their hopes; and then how the brave Canning for nine days and nights dragged the bottom of the ocean for our lost treasure, and, though he grappled it three times, failed to bring it to the surface. The story of that expedition, as written by Dr. Russell, who was on board the "Great Eastern," is one of the most marvelous chapters in the whole history of modern enterprise. We returned to England defeated, yet full of resolution to begin the battle anew. Measures were at once taken to make a second cable and fit out a new expedition; and with that assurance I came home to New York in the autumn.

In December I went back again, when lo! all our hopes had sunk to nothing. The Attorney-General of England had given his written opinion that we had no legal right, without a special act of Parliament (which could not be obtained under a year), to issue the new 12 per cent. shares, on which we relied to raise our capital. This was a terrible blow. The works were at once stopped, and the money which had been paid in returned to the subscribers. Such was the state of things when I reached London on December 24, 1865, and the next day was not a "merry" Christmas to me. But it was an inexpressible comfort to have the counsel of such men as Sir Daniel Gooch and Sir Richard A. Glass, and to hear stout-hearted Mr. Brassey tell us to go ahead, and, if need were, he would put down sixty thousand pounds more. It was finally concluded that the best course was to organize a new company, which should assume the work; and so originated the Anglo-American Telegraph Company. It was formed by ten gentlemen who met around a table in London and put down ten thousand pounds apiece. The great Telegraph Construction and Maintenance Company, undaunted by the failure of last year, answered us with a subscription of one hundred thousand pounds. Soon after the books were opened to the public, through the eminent banking-house of J. S. Morgan and Company, and in fourteen days we had raised the six hundred thousand pounds. Then the work began again, and went on with speed. Never was greater energy infused into any enterprise. It was only the last day of March that the new company was formed, and it was registered as a company the next day; and yet such was the vigor and dispatch that in five months from that day the cable had been manufactured, shipped on the "Great Eastern," stretched across the

LAYING THE FIRST SUCCESSFUL CABLE 27

Atlantic, and was sending messages, literally swift as lightning, from continent to continent.

Yet this was not "a lucky hit"—a fine run across the ocean in calm weather. It was the worst weather I ever knew at that season of the year. The dispatch that appeared in the New York papers read, "The weather has been most pleasant." I wrote it "unpleasant." We had fogs and storms almost the whole way. Our success was the result of the highest science combined with practical experience. Everything was perfectly organized to the minutest detail.

But our work was not over. After landing the cable safely at Newfoundland, we had another task—to return to mid-ocean and recover that lost in the expedition of last year. This achievement has perhaps excited more surprise than the other. Many even now "don't understand it," and every day I am asked "How it was done?" Well, it does seem rather difficult to fish for a jewel at the bottom of the ocean two and a half miles deep. But it is not so very difficult when you know how. You may be sure we did not go fishing at random, nor was our success mere "luck." It was the triumph of the highest nautical and engineering skill. We had four ships, and on board of them some of the best seamen in England —men who knew the ocean as a hunter knows every trail in the forest. There was Captain Moriarty, who was in the "Agamemnon" in 1857-1858. He was in the "Great Eastern" in 1865, and saw the cable when it broke; and he and Captain Anderson at once took observations so exact that they could go right to the spot. After finding it, they marked the line of the cable by buoys; for fogs would come, and shut out sun and stars, so that no man could take an observation.

These buoys were anchored a few miles apart, they were numbered, and each had a flagstaff on it so that it could be seen by day, and a lantern by night. Having thus taken our bearings, we stood off three or four miles, so as to come broadside on, and then, casting over the grapnel, drifted slowly down upon it, dragging the bottom of the ocean as we went. At first it was a little awkward to fish in such deep water, but our men got used to it, and soon could cast a grapnel almost as straight as an old whaler throws a harpoon. Our fishing line was a formidable size. It was made of rope, twisted with wires of steel, so as to bear a strain of thirty tons. It took about two hours for the grapnel to reach bottom, but we could tell when it struck. I often went to the bow, and sat on the rope, and could feel by the quiver that the grapnel was dragging on the bottom two miles under us. But it was a very slow business. We had storms and calms and fogs and squalls.

Still we worked on day after day. Once, on August 17th, we got the cable up, and had it in full sight for five minutes, a long, slimy monster, fresh from the ooze of the ocean's bed, but our men began to cheer so wildly that it seemed to be frightened and suddenly broke away and went down into the sea.

LAYING THE FIRST SUCCESSFUL CABLE   29

This accident kept us at work two weeks longer, but, finally, on the last night of August we caught it. We had cast the grapnel thirty times. It was a little before midnight on Friday night that we hooked the cable and it was a little after midnight Sunday morning when we got it on board. What was the anxiety of those twenty-six hours! The strain on every man was like the strain on the cable itself. When finally it appeared, it was midnight; the lights of the ship, and those in the boats around our bows, as they flashed in the faces of the men, showed them eagerly watching for the cable to appear on the water.

At length it was brought to the surface. All who were allowed to approach crowded forward to see it. Yet not a word was spoken save by the officers in command who were heard giving orders. All felt as if life and death hung on the issue. It was only when the cable was brought over the bow and on to the deck that men dared to breathe. Even then they hardly believed their eyes. Some crept toward it to feel of it, to be sure it was there. Then we carried it along to the electricians' room, to see if our long-sought-for treasure was alive or dead. A few minutes of suspense, and a flash told of the lightning current again set free. Then did the feeling long pent up burst forth. Some turned away their heads and wept. Others broke into cheers, and the cry ran from man to man, and was heard down in the engine-rooms, deck below deck, and from the boats on the water, and the other ships, while rockets lighted the darkness of the sea. Then with thankful hearts we turned our faces again to the west.

But soon the wind rose, and for thirty-six hours we were exposed to all the dangers of a storm on the Atlantic. Yet in the very height and fury of the gale, as I sat in the electricians' room, a flash of light came up from the deep, which, having crossed to Ireland, came back to me in mid-ocean, telling that those so dear to me, whom I had left on the bank of the Hudson, were well and following us with their wishes and their prayers. This was like a whisper of God from the sea, bidding me keep heart and hope. The "Great Eastern" bore herself proudly through the storm, as if she knew that the vital cord, which was to join two hemispheres, hung at her stern; and so, on Saturday, September 7th, we brought our second cable safely to the shore.

WHY THE UNITED STATES WANTED ALASKA

By Senator Charles Sumner

Although the purchase of Alaska was consummated by William H. Seward, as Secretary of State, Sumner, as chairman of the Senate Committee on Foreign Relations, was its chief sponsor in Congress. His speech upon the cession of Russian America to the United States, on April 9, 1867, was followed the next day by the vote in favor of ratification.

In this celebrated address he described to his less enlightened compeers the character and value of Alaska, comprising 590,000 square miles of territory, exceeding that of the original thirteen States and nearly one-sixth the area of the United States. Its coast line, including bays and islands, is greater than the circumference of the earth.

Subsequently Senator Sumner wrote out his speech for publication, and this is the main portion of it. It is taken from his collected "Works," by permission of the publishers, Lothrop, Lee & Shepard, Boston.

Advantages to the Pacific Coast.—Foremost in order, if not in importance, I put the desires of our fellow-citizens on the Pacific coast, and the special advantages they will derive from this enlargement of boundary. They were the first to ask for it, and will be the first to profit by it. While others knew the Russian possessions only on the map, they knew them practically on their own resources. While others were indifferent, they were planning how to appropriate Russian pelteries and fisheries. This is attested by the resolutions of the Legislature of Washington Territory; also by the exertions at different times of two Senators from California, who differing in political sentiments and in party relations, took the initial steps which ended in this treaty.

These well-known desires were founded, of course, on supposed advantages; and here experience and neighborhood were prompters. Since 1854 the people of California have received their ice from the fresh-water lakes in the island of Kadiak, not far westward from Mount St. Elias. Later still, their fishermen have searched the waters about the Aleutians and the Shumagins, commencing a promising fishery. Others have proposed to substitute themselves for the Hudson's Bay Company in their franchise on the coast. But all are looking to the Orient, as in the time of Columbus, although like him they sail to the west. To them China and Japan, those ancient realms of fabulous wealth, are the Indies.

The absence of harbors belonging to the United States on the Pacific limits the outlets of the country. On that whole extent, from Panama to Puget Sound, the only harbor of any considerable value is San Francisco. Farther north the harbors are abundant, and they are all nearer to the great marts of Japan and China. But San Francisco itself will be nearer by the way of the Aleutians than by Honolulu. . . .

The advantages to the Pacific coast have two aspects—domestic and foreign. Not only does the treaty extend the coasting trade of California, Oregon and Washington Territory northward, but it also extends the base of commerce with China and Japan.

To unite the East of Asia with the West of America is the aspiration of commerce now as when the English navigator recorded his voyage. Of course, whatever helps this result is an advantage. The Pacific Railroad is such an advantage; for, though running westward, it will be, when completed, a new highway to the East. This treaty is another advantage; for nothing can be clearer than that the western coast must exercise an attraction which will be felt in China and Japan just in proportion as it is occupied by a commercial people communicating readily with the Atlantic and with Europe. This cannot be without consequences not less important politically than commercially. Owing so much to the Union, the people there will be bound to it anew, and the national unity will receive another confirmation. Thus the whole country will be a gainer. So are we knit together that the advantages to the Pacific coast will contribute to the general welfare.

2. Extension of Dominion.—The extension of dominion is another consideration calculated to captivate the public mind. . . .

The passion for acquisition, so strong in the individual, is not less strong in the community. A nation seeks an outlying territory, as an individual seeks an outlying farm. . . . It is common to the human family. There are few anywhere who could hear of a considerable accession of territory, obtained peacefully and honestly, without a pride of country, even if at certain moments the judgment hesitated.

With increased size on the map there is increased consciousness of strength, and the heart of the citizen throbs anew as he traces the extending line.

3. Extension of Republican Institutions.—More than the extension of dominion is the extension of republican institutions, which is a traditional aspiration. . . .

John Adams, in the preface to his Defense of the American Constitutions written in London, where he resided at the time as Minister, and dated January 1, 1787, at Grosvenor Square, the central seat of aristocratic fashion, after exposing the fabulous origin of the kingly power in contrast with the simple origin of our republican constitutions, thus for a moment lifts the curtain: "Thirteen governments," he says plainly, "thus founded on the natural authority of the people alone, without a pretense of miracle or mystery, and which are destined to spread over the northern part of that whole quarter of the globe, are a great point gained in favor of the rights of mankind." Thus, according to the prophetic Minister, even at that early day was the detesting of the Republic manifest. It was to spread over the northern part of the American quarter of the globe, and it was to help the rights of mankind.

By the text of our Constitution, the United States are bound to guaranty "a republican form of government" to every State in the Union; but this obligation, which is applicable only at home, is an unquestionable indication of the national aspiration every-

WHY THE UNITED STATES WANTED ALASKA   35

where. The Republic is something more than a local policy; it is a general principle, not to be forgotten at any time, especially when the opportunity is presented of bringing an immense region within its influence. . . .

The present treaty is a visible step in the occupation of the whole North American continent. As such it will be recognized by the world and accepted by the American people. But the treaty involves something more. We dismiss one other monarch from the continent. One by one they have retired, —first France, then Spain, then France again, and now Russia,—all giving way to the absorbing Unity declared in the national motto, "E pluribus unum."

4. Anticipation of Great Britain.—Another motive to this acquisition may be found in the desire to anticipate imagined schemes or necessities of Great Britain. With regard to all these I confess doubt; and yet, if we credit report, it would seem as if there were already a British movement in this direction. Sometimes it is said that Great Britain desires to buy, if Russia will sell. . . .

5. Amity of Russia.—There is still another consideration concerning this treaty not to be disregarded. It attests and assures the amity of Russia. Even if you doubt the value of these possessions, the treaty is a sign of friendship. It is a new expression of that "entente cordiale" between the two powers which is a phenomenon of history. Though unlike in institutions, they are not unlike in recent experi-

ence. Sharers of common glory in a great act of Emancipation, they also share together the opposition or antipathy of other nations. Perhaps this experience has not been without effect in bringing them together. At all events, no coldness or unkindness has interfered at any time with their good relations.

. . . The Rebellion, which tempted so many other powers into its embrace, could not draw Russia from her habitual good-will. Her solicitude for the Union was early declared. She made no unjustifiable concession of ocean belligerence, with all its immunities and powers, to rebels in arms against the Union. She furnished no hospitality to rebel cruisers, nor was any rebel agent ever received, entertained, or encouraged at St. Petersburg,—while, on the other hand, there was an understanding that the United States should be at liberty to carry prizes into Russian ports. So natural and easy were the relations between the two Governments, that such complaints as incidentally arose on either side were amicably adjusted by verbal explanations without written controversy. . . .

In relations such as I have described, the cession of territory seems a natural transaction, entirely in harmony with the past. It remains to hope that it may be a new link in an amity which, without effort, has overcome differences of institutions and intervening space on the globe. . . .

At all events, now that the treaty has been signed by plenipotentiaries on each side duly empowered, it is difficult to see how we can refuse to complete the purchase without putting to hazard the friendly relations which happily subsist between the United States and Russia. The overtures originally proceeded from us. After a delay of years, and other intervening propositions, the bargain was at length concluded. It is with nations as with individuals. A bargain once made must be kept. Even if still open to consideration, it must not be lightly abandoned. I am satisfied that the dishonoring of this treaty, after what has passed, would be a serious responsibility for our country. As an international question, it would be tried by the public opinion of the world; and there are many who, not appreciating the requirement of our Constitution by which a treaty must have "the advice and consent of the Senate," would regard its rejection as bad faith. There would be jeers at us, and jeers at Russia also: at us for levity in making overtures, and at Russia for levity in yielding to them. Had the Senate been consulted in advance, before the treaty was signed or either power publicly committed, as is often done on important occasions, it would be under less constraint. On such a consultation there would have been opportunity for all possible objections, and a large latitude for reasonable discretion. Let me add that, while forbearing objection now, I hope that this treaty may not be drawn into a precedent, at least in the independent manner of its negotiations. I would save to the Senate an important power justly belonging to it.

THE PURCHASE OF ALASKA

By Frederic Bancroft

SEWARD not only regarded the purchase of Alaska from Russia, in 1867, as of the highest value and significance, but he believed it was the destiny of the United States to incorporate the whole of North America, with the City of Mexico as the ultimate capital of the Republic. Asked what he considered the most important act of his political career, he replied: "The purchase of Alaska; but it will take the people a generation to find it out." As early as 1846 he said: "Our population is destined to roll its resistless waves to the icy barriers of the North, and to encounter Oriental civilization on the Pacific."

Two years after the transaction, here recounted by Frederic Bancroft in his "Life of Seward," the imperialistic Secretary of State visited what was called "Seward's Arctic Province," and at Sitka made a memorable address expressing his impressions of the $7,200,000 purchase.

THE purchase of Alaska has often been called Seward's greatest service to his country. A vast territory which Russia acquired by right of discovery and held for considerably more than a century was sold to the United States before hardly a dozen Americans knew that such a proposition was even under consideration. There is a tradition that during Polk's administration something was said to Russia about parting with her possessions in North America. It is certain that as early as 1859 Senator Gwin and the Assistant Secretary of State discussed the question with Stoeckl, the Russian Minister at Washington, and that as much as five million dollars was offered. The official answer was that this sum was not regarded as adequate, but that Russia would be ready to carry on negotiations as soon as the Minister of Finance could look into the question. There was no occasion for haste; Buchanan soon went out of office; and the subject, which was never known to many persons, seems to have been entirely forgotten for several years.

The interests of a few citizens on the Pacific slope were the mainspring of the little that had been done. For more than a decade San Francisco had annually received a large amount of ice from Russian America, and United States fishermen had been profitably engaged in different parts of the far northern Pacific. Those interests had rapidly increased from year to year. At the beginning of 1866 the legislature of Washington Territory sent a petition to President Johnson, saying that an abundance of codfish, halibut and salmon had been found along the shores of Russian America, and requesting him to obtain from the Russian government such concessions as would enable American fishing vessels to visit the ports and harbors of that region for the purpose of obtaining fuel, water and provisions. Sumner says that this was referred to the Secretary of State, who suggested to Stoeckl that some comprehensive arrangement should be made to prevent any difficulties arising between the United States and Russia on account of the fisheries. About this time several Californians wished to obtain a franchise to carry on the fur-trade in Russian America. Senator Cole, of California, urged both

Seward and Stoeckl to support the request. Seward instructed Cassius M. Clay, the United States Minister at St. Petersburg, to consult the Russian government on the subject. Clay reported on February, 1867, that there was a prospect of success. In fact, the time happened to be peculiarly opportune for negotiation.

Russian America had never been brought under the regular rule of the imperial government. Since the beginning of the century its few thousand civilized inhabitants had been governed by a great monopoly called the Russian-American Company. Its charter had expired with the year 1861, and had not been renewed; yet a renewal was expected. This monopoly was so unprofitable that it had sought and obtained special privileges, such as the free importation of tea into Russia. It had even sublet some of its privileges to the Hudson Bay Company. This sublease to Englishmen was to expire in June, 1867. By the usual means of communication Russian America was from Russia one of the most distant regions on earth. To organize it as a colony would involve great expense and continuous financial loss. To defend it in time of war with Great Britain or the United States would be an impossibility. When the Crimean war broke out common interest led the Russian-American and the Hudson Bay companies to induce their respective governments to neutralize the Russian and the British possessions on the northwest coast of America. Otherwise Great Britain might easily have seized the Russian Territory. To the imperial government at

THE PURCHASE OF ALASKA

the beginning of 1867 the problem resolved itself into these three questions: Shall the charter of the monopoly, with its privileges and unsatisfactory treatment of the inhabitants, be renewed? Shall an expensive colonial system be organized? Shall we sell at a fair price territory that will surely be lost, if it ever becomes populated and valuable? It was foreseen that unless sold to the most constant and grateful of Russia's friends, it was likely to be taken by her strongest and most inveterate enemy. Stoeckl was spending part of the winter of 1866-67 in St. Petersburg, and the different questions were talked over with him, for he had long been Minister to the United States. In February, 1867, as he was about to return to Washington, "the Archduke Constantine, the brother and chief adviser of the Emperor, handed him a map with the lines in our treaty marked upon it, and told him he might treat for this cession."

The following month Stoeckl and Seward began negotiations. One named ten million dollars as a reasonable price; the other offered five millions. Then they took the middle ground—namely, seven million five hundred thousand—as a basis. Seward urged and Stoeckl agreed that the half million should be dropped. The Russian-American Company still claimed privileges and held interests that could not be ignored. Seward saw the objections to assuming any responsibility for matters of this kind; so he offered to add two hundred thousand dollars to the seven millions if Russia would give a title free from all liabilities. On the evening of March 29, 1867, the Russian Minister called at Seward's house and informed him of the receipt of a cablegram reporting the Emperor's consent to the proposition, and then he added that he would be ready to take up the final work the next day, for haste was desirable. With a smile of satisfaction at the news, Seward pushed aside the table where he had been enjoying his usual evening game of whist, and said: "Why wait until tomorrow, Mr. Stoeckl? Let us make the treaty to-night." The needed clerks were summoned; the Assistant Secretary went after Sumner, the chairman of the Senate Committee on Foreign Affairs; the Russian Minister sent for his assistants; and at midnight all met at the Department of State. By four o'clock in the morning the task was completed. In a few hours the President sent the treaty to the Senate.

HUNTING BUFFALO TO FEED THE RAILROAD BUILDERS

By William F. (Buffalo Bill) Cody

"COLONEL" CODY, better known as "Buffalo Bill," was the last of the line of great American scouts. In his "True Tales of the Plains" (Harper & Brothers) he gives this account of his buffalo-hunting exploits. He gained his sobriquet as a hunter engaged, in 1867, to furnish buffalo-meat to the laborers at work on what is now the Union Pacific Railroad. In a twelvemonth, as here recorded, he killed 4,280 bison, 69 of them in one day. Later he was made chief of United States Army scouts by General Sheridan, then campaigning against the Indians, and in 1876 he slew Chief Yellow Hand in a celebrated personal encounter during the Sioux War.

With his picturesque "Wild West Show," he toured America and Europe for many years, accumulating a fortune which he invested in land embracing the present site of Cody, Wyoming. Dying in 1917, his picturesque grave is on a Colorado mountaintop near Denver.

ONE of my favorite buffalo-hunting horses was a small roan or large Indian pony which I got from a Ute Indian. As this horse came from Utah I named him "Brigham," after the Mormon prophet, Brigham Young. During the construction of the Kansas Pacific Railroad (now the Union Pacific), in 1867, the construction of the end of the track got into the great buffalo country, and at that time the Indians—the Sioux, Cheyennes, Comanches and Arapahoes—were all on the war-path. It was before the railway refrigerator car was in use and the contractors had no fresh meat to feed their employees. The men were grumbling considerably for fresh meat, for they could see fresh meat—that is, the buffalo, deer and antelope—in every direction, and they would growl because the contractors did not kill the buffaloes so that they could have fresh meat to eat. This was a little more difficult job than they thought, as the Indians were contesting every mile of railroad that was being built into their country. Besides having military escorts to guard the graders every man from the boss down who went to work on the grading of the road carried a rifle with him as well as a pick and shovel, and when he was using them his gun lay on the ground near him, as the Indians would daily attack them.

The construction of that road, in 1867, was nearly a continuous fight, and it was dangerous for a man to venture any distance away from the troops and the graders to hunt the buffalo. They tried several hunters who claimed that they could kill buffalo and bring it into camp so that they could have fresh meat for their men. One or two of these men were killed by Indians while doing so, and the others gave up the job.

At that time I was guide and scout at Fort Hays, Kansas, and had quite a reputation as a buffalo hunter. Some one told the main contractor that if he could get me I would be able to kill all the buffalo he would require. He came to Fort Hays to see me. Of course I could not accept—although he made me a very tempting financial offer—without permission of the Military Department Commander, General Sheridan.

FEEDING THE RAILROAD BUILDERS

The subject was even discussed at headquarters in Washington, and, after considerable delay, evidence was presented that it would solve one of the main labor problems in the great work of constructing the transcontinental railroad and facilitate matters greatly. Leave of absence for the purpose was given me, with the understanding that in case of an important outbreak I should resume the duties of my position. As roving Indians generally followed the herds of buffalo, I was really in a certain sense performing scouting duty also.

I started in killing buffalo for the Union Pacific Railroad. I had a wagon with four mules, one driver and two butchers, all brave, well-armed men, myself riding my horse "Brigham." We could leave the end of the construction work to go out after buffalo, and had an understanding with the commanding officer who had charge of the troops guarding the construction that, should a smoke signal be seen in the direction in which I had gone, they would know I was in trouble and would send mounted men to my assistance.

I had to keep a close and careful lookout for Indians before making my run into a herd of buffalo. It was my custom in those days to pick out a herd that seemed to have the fattest cows and young heifers. I would then rush my horse into them, picking out the fattest cows and shooting them down, while my horse would be running alongside of them. I had a happy faculty in knowing how to shoot down the leaders and get the herd to run in a circle. I have killed from twenty-five to forty buffalo while the herd was circling, and they would all be dropped very close together; that is to say, in a space covering about five acres. When I had the number I wanted, I would stop shooting and allow the balance of the herd to get away. The wagon would drive up and my men would instantly begin to secure the hams, the tenderloins, the tongues, and the choicest meat of each buffalo, including the heads, which were afterward mounted and used for advertisement for the said road, loading the wagon until it was full. We would then drive back to our camp, or to the end of the track where the men were at work, and when the men would see me coming with a load of fresh meat they would say: "Ah, here comes Bill with a lot of nice buffalo!" For a while they were delighted with the fresh tender meat, but after a time they tired of it, and, seeing me come would say: "Here comes this old Bill with more buffalo!" and finally they connected the name buffalo and Bill together, and that is where the foundation was laid to the name of "Buffalo Bill," which afterward I defended as a title with Comstock before the officers at Fort Wallace with success.

I killed buffalo for the railroad company for twelve months, and during that time the number I brought into camp was kept account of, and at the end of that period I had killed 4,280 buffalo on old "Brigham."

FEEDING THE RAILROAD BUILDERS 47

This was all accomplished with one needle-gun or breech-loader, which I named "Lucretia Borgia."

During those twelve months I had many fights with the Indians. On several occasions they "jumped" myself and little party while several miles from the end of the grade. We would always prefer to have them "jump" us after our wagon was loaded with buffalo hams, for we had rehearsed our little stockade so often that it did not take more than a few minutes from the time we saw them coming until the mules were unhitched from the wagon and tied to the wheels. We would make our breastwork around the wheels of the wagon by throwing out the meat, and would protect ourselves by getting behind the buffalo hams. In this manner we held off from forty to sixty Indians on one or two occasions until we received assistance. I would make my smoke signals at once, which the soldiers would instantly see and rush to our rescue. I had five men killed during my connection with the U. P. R. R., three drivers and the others butchers.

THE THREATENED IMPEACHMENT OF ANDREW JOHNSON

By Senator Shelby M. Cullom

SENATOR CULLOM, from whose "Fifty Years of Public Service" this account is taken, by permission of A. C. McClurg & Company, was a member of Congress from Illinois at the time impeachment proceedings were brought against President Andrew Johnson.

Leading up to the threatened impeachment of Johnson, which was averted in the Senate by the narrow margin of one vote less than the two-thirds necessary, Congress had repassed several bills over the President's veto. In August, 1867, Stanton was displaced by General Grant as Secretary of War. A month later Congress refused to ratify Stanton's suspension, whereupon Grant resigned and Stanton resumed his post. Early in 1868 Johnson again removed Stanton, and put General Lorenzo Thomas in his place, thereby provoking the historic impeachment proceedings, which Cullom supported.

AS I look back now over the vista of the years that have come and gone, it seems to me that I entered the Lower House of Congress just at the beginning of the most important period in all our history. The great President had been assassinated; the war was over; Andrew Johnson, a Union Democrat, was President of the United States. Reconstruction was the problem which confronted us, how to heal up the nation's wounds and remake a Union which would endure for all time to come. These were the difficult conditions that had to be dealt with by the Thirty-ninth Congress.

Andrew Johnson was the queerest character that ever occupied the White House, and, with the exception of Lincoln only, he entered it under the most trying and difficult circumstances in all our history; but Lincoln had, what Johnson lacked, the support and confidence of the great Republican party. Johnson was never a Republican, and never pretended to be one. He was a lifelong Democrat, and a slaveholder as well; but he was loyal to the Union, no man living more so. As a Senator from Tennessee, alone of all the Southern Senators, he faced his colleagues from the South in denouncing secession as treason. His subsequent phenomenal course in armed opposition to the Rebellion brought about his nomination for the Vice-Presidency as a shrewd stroke to secure the support of the War Democrats of the North and the Union men of his State and section. . . .

. . . The scene which took place in the Senate chamber when Johnson was inducted into office as Vice-President; the exhibition he made of himself at the time of taking the oath of office, in the presence of the President of the United States, and the representatives of the governments of the world—all this, advertised at the time in the opposition press, added to the prejudice against Johnson in the North and made his position more trying and difficult.

There were two striking points in Johnson's character, and I knew him well: first, his loyalty to the Union; and, second, his utter fearlessness of character. He could not be cowed; old Ben Wade, Sumner, Stevens, all the great leaders of that day could not, through fear, influence him one particle.

In 1861, when he was being made the target of all sorts of threats on account of his solitary stand against secession in the Senate, he let fall this characteristic utterance: "I want to say, not boastingly, with no anger in my bosom, that these two eyes of mine have never looked upon anything in the shape of mortal man that this heart has feared." This utterance probably illustrates Johnson's character more clearly than anything that I could say. He sought rather than avoided a fight. Headstrong, domineering, having fought his way in a State filled with aristocratic Southerners, from the class of so-called "low whites" to the highest position in the United States, he did not readily yield to the dictates of the dominating forces in Congress.

Lincoln had a well-defined policy of reconstruction. Indeed, so liberal was he disposed to be in his treatment of the Southern States that immediately after the surrender of Richmond he would have recognized the old State Government of Virginia had it not been for the peremptory veto of Stanton. Congress was not in session when Johnson came to the Presidency in April, 1865. To do him no more than simple justice, I firmly believe that he wanted to follow out, in reconstruction, what he thought was the policy of Mr. Lincoln, and in this he was guided largely by the advice of Mr. Seward.

But there was this difference. Johnson was, probably in good faith, pursuing the Lincoln policy of reconstruction; but when the legislatures and executives of the Southern States began openly passing laws and executing them so that the negro was substantially placed back into slavery, practically nullifying the results of the awful struggle, the untold loss of life and treasure, Mr. Lincoln certainly would have receded and would have dealt with the South with an iron hand, as Congress had determined to do, and as General Grant was compelled to do when he assumed the Presidency.

From April to the reassembling of Congress in December, Johnson had a free hand in dealing with the seceding States, and he was not slow to take advantage of it. He seemed disposed to recognize the old State governments; to restrict the suffrage to the whites; to exercise freely the pardoning power in the way of extending executive clemency not only to almost all classes, but to every individual who would apply for it. The result was, it seemed to be certain that if the Johnson policy were carried out to the fullest extent the supremacy of the Republican party in the councils of the nation would be at stake.

To express it in a word, the motive of the opposition to the Johnson plan of reconstruction was the firm conviction that its success would wreck the Republican party, and by restoring the Democrats to power bring back Southern supremacy and Northern vassalage. The impeachment, in a word, was a culmination of the struggle between the legislative and the executive departments of the Government over the problem of reconstruction. The legislative department claimed exclusive jurisdiction over reconstruction; the executive claimed that it alone was competent to deal with the subject. . . .

It was at once determined by the Republican majority in Congress that the representatives of the eleven seceding States should not be admitted. The Constitution expressly gives to the House and Senate the exclusive power to judge of the admission and qualification of its own members.

We were surprised at the moderation of the President's message, which came in on Tuesday after Congress assembled. In tone and general character the message was wholly unlike Johnson. It was an admirable state document, one of the finest from a literary and probably from every other standpoint that ever came from an executive to Congress. It was thought at the time that Mr. Seward wrote it, but it has since been asserted that it was the product of that foremost of American historians [George] Bancroft, one of Mr. Johnson's close personal friends.

There existed three theories of dealing with the Southern States; one was the President's theory of recognizing the State governments, allowing the States to deal with the suffrage question as they might see fit; the Stevens policy of wiping out all State lines and dealing with the regions as conquered military provinces; and the Sumner theory of treating them as organized territories, recognizing the State lines. . . .

What determined Johnson in his course, I do not know. It was thought that he would be a radical of radicals. Being of the "poor white" class, he may have been flattered by the attentions showered on him by the old Southern aristocrats. Writers of this period have frequently given that as a reason. My own belief has been that he was far too strong a man to be governed in so vital a matter by so trivial a cause. My conviction is that the radical Republican leaders in the House were right; that he believed in the old Democratic party, aside from his loyalty to the Union; and was a Democrat determined to turn the Government over to the Democratic party, reconstructed on a Union basis.

I cannot undertake to go into all the long details of that memorable struggle. As I look back over the history of it now, it seems to me to bear a close resemblance to the beginning of the French Revolution, to the struggle between the States General of France and Louis XVI. Might we not, if things had turned differently, have drifted into chaos and revolution? If Johnson had been impeached and refused to submit, adopting the same tactics as did Stanton in retaining the War Department; had Ben Wade taken the oath of office and demanded possession, Heaven only knows what might have been the result.

But reminiscing in this way, as I cannot avoid doing when I think back over those terrible times, I lose the continuity of my subject. An extension to the Freedman's Bureau bill was passed, was promptly vetoed by the Executive, the veto was as promptly overruled by the House, where there was no substantial opposition, but the Senate failed to pass the bill, the veto of the President to the contrary notwithstanding.

I had not the remotest idea that Johnson would dare to veto the Freedman's Bureau bill, and I made a speech on the subject, declaring a firm conviction to that effect. A veto at that time was almost unheard of. Except during the administration of Tyler, no important bill had ever been vetoed by an executive. It came as a shock to Congress and the country. Excitement reigned supreme. The question was, "Should the bill pass the veto of the President regardless thereof?"

Not the slightest difficulty existed in the House; Thaddeus Stevens had too complete control of that body to allow any question concerning it there. The bill, therefore, was promptly passed over the veto of the President. But the situation in the Senate was different. At that time the Sumner-Wade radical element did not have the necessary two-thirds majority, and the bill failed to pass over the veto of the President. The war between the executive and legislative departments of the Government had fairly commenced, and the first victory had been won by the President.

The Civil Rights bill, drawn and introduced by Judge Trumbull, than whom there was no greater lawyer in the United States Senate, in January, 1866, on the reassembling of Congress, was passed. Then began the real struggle on the part of the radicals in

THREATENED IMPEACHMENT OF JOHNSON 55

the Senate, headed by Sumner and Wade, to muster the necessary two-thirds majority to pass a bill over the veto of the President.

Let me digress here to say a word in reference to Charles Sumner. . . . It was his mission to awake the public conscience to the horrors of slavery. He performed his duty unfalteringly, and it almost cost him his life. Mr. Lincoln was the only man living who ever managed Charles Sumner, or could use him for his purpose. Sumner's end has always seemed to me most pitiful. Removed from his high position as chairman of the Foreign Relations Committee of the Senate, followed relentlessly by the enmity of President Grant, then at the very acme of his fame; drifting from the Republican party, his own State repudiating him, Charles Sumner died of a broken heart.

But to return to the struggle between the President and Congress. Trumbull, Sumner, Wade and the leaders were bound in one way or another to get the necessary two-thirds. The vote was taken in the Senate: "Shall the Civil Rights bill pass the veto of the President to the contrary notwithstanding?" It was understood the vote would be very close, and the result uncertain.

The excitement was intense. The galleries were crowded; members of the House were on the Senate floor. The result seemed to depend entirely on the vote of Senator Morgan, of New York, and he seemed to be irresolute, uncertain in his own mind which way he would vote. The call of the roll proceeded. When his name was reached there was profound silence. He first voted nay, and then immediately changed to yea. A wonderful demonstration burst forth, as it was then known that the bill would pass over the veto of the President, and that the Republican party in Congress at last had complete control. Senator Trumbull made a remarkable speech on that occasion, and I was never prouder of any living man.

So the struggle went on from day to day and year to year, growing all the time more intense. I have always been disposed to be conservative; I was then; and it was with profound regret that I saw the feeling between the President and Congress becoming more and more strained.

I disliked to follow the extreme radical element, and when the row was at its height, Judge Orth, a colleague in the House from Indiana, and I concluded to go and see the President and advise with him, in an attempt to smooth over the differences. I will never forget that interview. It was at night. He received us politely enough, and without mincing any words he gave us to understand that we were on a fool's errand and that he would not yield. We went away, and naturally joined the extreme radicals in the House, always voting with them afterward.

The row continued in the Fortieth Congress. Bills were passed, promptly vetoed, and the bills immediately passed over the President's veto. Many of the bills were not only unwise legislation, but were unconstitutional as well. We passed the Tenure of Office bill; we attempted to restrict the President's pardoning power; and as I look back over the history of the period, it seems to me that we did not have the slightest regard for the Constitution. Some of President Johnson's veto messages were admirable. He had the advice and assistance of one of the ablest lawyers of his day, Jeremiah Black.

To make the feeling more intense, just about this time Johnson made his famous "swing around the circle," as it was termed. His speeches published in the opposition press were intemperate and extreme. He denounced Congress. He threatened to "kick people out of office," in violation of the Tenure of Office act. He was undignified in his actions and language, and many people thought he was intoxicated most of the time, although I do not believe this.

The radicals in both the House and Senate determined that he should be impeached and removed from office. They had the votes in the House easily, and they thought they could muster the necessary number in the Senate, as we had been passing all sorts of legislation over the President's veto. When the subject was up, I was doubtful, and I really believe, strong Republican that I was, that had it not been for Judge Trumbull I would have voted against the impeachment articles. I advised with the judge, for whom I had profound respect. I visited him at his house. I explained to him my doubts, and I recall very clearly the expression he used in reply. He said: "Johnson is an obstruction to the Government, and should be removed." Judge Trumbull himself changed afterward much to the astonishment of every one, and denounced the impeachment proceeding as unworthy of a justice of the peace court.

It seems to me difficult to realize that it was as far back as March 2, 1868, that I addressed the House in favor of the impeachment articles. I think I made a pretty good speech on that occasion and supported my position very well. I took rather an extreme view in favor of the predominance of the legislative department of the Government, contending that the executive and judiciary departments of the Government, while they are finally responsible to the people, are directly accountable to the legislative department.

The first and principal article in the impeachment proposed by the House was the President's issuance of an order removing Edwin M. Stanton as Secretary of War, he having been duly appointed and commissioned by and with the advice and consent of the Senate, and the Senate having been in session at the time of his removal. I contended then, on the floor of the House, that such a removal was a violation of the Constitution, and could not be excused on any pretext whatever, in addition to being a direct violation of the Tenure of Office act.

I do not intend to go into the details of the various articles proposed by the House; suffice it to say that they were mainly based on the attempted removal

THREATENED IMPEACHMENT OF JOHNSON 59

of Mr. Stanton, and the appointment of Mr. Thomas as Secretary of War. . . .

Needless for me to say, as the subject continued feeling remained at a high pitch in the House. It was debated from day to day. Stevens was urging the impeachment with all the force at his command; some were doubtful and holding back, as I was; some changed—for instance, James G. Blaine, who was taunted by Stevens and sneered at for his change of front.

Under the law then existing the President of the Senate succeeded a Vice-President who became, by the death or removal of the President, President of the United States. The radicals in complete control —and I have no doubt that Stevens had a hand in it —elected the most radical of their number as President of the Senate—Ben Wade, of Ohio. Johnson removed, Wade would have been President, and the extreme radicals would have been in supreme control of the legislative and executive departments of the Government.

This condition is what made Mr. Blaine hesitate. He told me on one occasion: "Johnson in the White House is bad enough, but we know what we have; Lord knows what we would get with old Ben Wade there. I do not know but I would rather trust Johnson than Wade." But in the end Blaine supported the impeachment articles, just as I did, and as Senator Allison and other somewhat conservative members did, all feeling at the same time not a little doubtful of our course.

Stevens, Logan, Boutwell, Williams and Wilson were appointed managers on the part of the House, and solemnly and officially notified the Senate of the action of the House in impeaching the President of the United States. The Senate proceeded without long delay to resolve itself as a High Court of Impeachment, for the purpose of trying the President of the United States for high crimes and misdemeanors. The most eminent counsel of the nation were engaged. Mr. Evarts was President Johnson's principal counsel. He was ably assisted by lawyers of scarcely less renown.

The trial dragged along from day to day. Part of the time the Senate considered the matter in executive session. The corridors were crowded; and I remember with what astonishment we heard that Judge Trumbull had taken the floor denouncing the proceeding as unworthy of a justice of the peace court. The Illinois delegation held a meeting, and Logan, Farnsworth and Washburne urged that we unite in a letter to Judge Trumbull, with a view to influencing his vote for conviction, or of inducing him to withhold his vote if he could not vote for conviction. A number of our delegation opposed it, and the letter was not sent.

I do not think that it would have made the slightest effect on Judge Trumbull had we sent it. All sorts of coercing methods were used to influence wavering

THREATENED IMPEACHMENT OF JOHNSON

Senators. Old Bob Schenck was the chairman of this movement, and he sent telegrams broadcast all over the United States to the effect that there was great danger to the peace of the country and the Republican cause if impeachment failed, and asking the recipients to send to their Senators public opinion by resolutions and delegations. And responses came from all over the North, urging and demanding the impeachment of the President.

It is difficult now to realize the intense excitement of that period. General Grant was there, tacitly acknowledged as the next nominee of the Republican party for the Presidency. He took no active part, but it was pretty well understood, from the position of his friends such as Logan and Washburne, that the impeachment had his sympathy; and in the Senate Conkling was especially vindictive. Grimes, Fessenden, and Trumbull led the fight for acquittal. Many were noncommittal; but in the end the struggle turned on the one doubtful Senator, Edmund G. Ross of Kansas.

It was determined to vote on the tenth article first, as that article was the strongest one and more votes could be mustered for it than any other. It was well understood that the vote on that article would settle the matter.

More than forty-three years have passed into history since that memorable day when the Senate of the United States was sitting as a Court of Impeachment for the purpose of trying the President of the United

States for high crimes and misdemeanors. The occasion is unforgettable. As I look back now, I see arising before me the forms and features of the great men who were sitting in that high court: I see presiding Chief Justice Chase; I see Sumner, cold and dignified; Wade, Trumbull, Hendricks, Conkling, Yates; I see Logan as one of the managers on the part of the House; I see old Thad Stevens, weak and wasted from illness, being carried in—all long since have passed to the beyond, the accused President, the members of the high court, the counsel. Of all the eminent men who were present on that day, aside from the Honorable J. B. Henderson, I do not know of a single one now living.

As the roll was called, there was such a solemn hush as only comes when man stands in the presence of Deity. Finally, when the name of Ross was reached and he voted "No"; when it was understood that his vote meant acquittal, the friends of the President in the galleries thundered forth in applause.

And thus ended for the first, and I hope the last, time the trial of a President of the United States before the Senate, sitting as a Court of Impeachment for high crimes and misdemeanors.

THE FOURTEENTH AMENDMENT

By Representative Thaddeus Stevens

STEVENS was the recognized leader of the radical Republicans in Congress from 1859 until his death in 1868. It was Stevens who reported the fourteenth amendment to the Constitution, giving the negroes citizenship. At that time he was chairman of the important House Reconstruction Committee. After the House had passed the amendment the Senate modified it, greatly to his disapproval.

Stevens and Johnson were bitter political enemies, and it was the former who was mainly responsible for the impeachment proceedings against President Johnson. Stevens was intolerant of compromises. During the Civil War, as chairman of the Committee on Ways and Means, he was as prompt and unsparing in helping the Federal Government meet its financial obligations as he afterwards was in condemning "rebels, traitors and copperheads." His theory of reconstruction was that the Southern States had forfeited all their rights, and being guilty of treason merited no mercy.

THIS proposition is not all that the committee desired. It falls far short of my wishes, but it fulfills my hopes. I believe it is all that can be obtained in the present state of public opinion. Not only Congress but the several States are to be consulted. Upon a careful survey of the whole ground, we did not believe that nineteen of the loyal States could be induced to ratify any proposition more stringent than this. I say nineteen, for I utterly repudiate and scorn the idea that any State not acting in the Union is to be counted on the question of ratification. It is absurd to suppose that any more than three-fourths of the States that propose the amendment are required to make it valid; that States not here are to be counted as present. Believing then, that this is the best proposition that can be made effectual, I accept it. . . .

The first section prohibits the States from abridging the privileges and immunities of citizens of the United States, or unlawfully depriving them of life, liberty, or property, or of denying to any person within their jurisdiction the "equal" protection of the laws.

I can hardly believe that any person can be found who will not admit that every one of these provisions is just. They are all asserted, in some form or other, in our Declaration or organic law. But the Constitution limits only the action of Congress, and is not a limitation on the States. This amendment supplies that defect, and allows Congress to correct the unjust legislation of the States, so far that the law which operates upon one man shall operate equally upon all. Whatever law punishes a white man for a crime shall punish the black man precisely in the same way and to the same degree. Whatever law protects the white man shall afford "equal" protection to the black man. Whatever means of redress is afforded to one shall be afforded to all. Whatever law allows the white man to testify in court shall allow the man of color to do the same. These are great advantages over their present codes. Now different degrees of punishment are inflicted, not on account of the magnitude of the crime, but according to the color of the skin. Now color disqualifies a man from testifying in courts, or being tried in the same way as white men.

THE FOURTEENTH AMENDMENT

I need not enumerate these partial and oppressive laws. Unless the Constitution should restrain them those States will all, I fear, keep up this discrimination, and crush to death the hated freedmen. Some answer, "Your civil rights bill secures the same things." That is partly true, but a law is repealable by a majority. And I need hardly say that the first time that the South with their copperhead allies obtain the command of Congress it will be repealed. The veto of the President and their votes on the bill are conclusive evidence of that. And yet I am amazed and alarmed at the impatience of certain well-meaning Republicans at the exclusion of the rebel States until the Constitution shall be so amended as to restrain their despotic desires. This amendment once adopted cannot be annulled without two-thirds of Congress. That they will hardly get. And yet certain of our distinguished friends propose to admit State after State before this becomes a part of the Constitution. What madness! Is their judgment misled by their kindness; or are they unconsciously drifting into the haven of power at the other end of the avenue? I do not suspect it, but others will.

The second section I consider the most important in the article. It fixes the basis of representation in Congress. If any State shall exclude any of her adult male citizens from the elective franchise, or abridge that right, she shall forfeit her right to representation in the same proportion. The effect of this provision will be either to compel the States to grant universal suffrage or so to shear them of their power as to keep them forever in a hopeless minority in the national Government, both legislative and executive. If they do not enfranchise the freedmen, it would give to the rebel States but thirty-seven Representatives. Thus shorn of their power, they would soon become restive. Southern pride would not long brook a hopeless minority. True it will take two, three, possibly five years before they conquer their prejudices sufficiently to allow their late slaves to become their equals at the polls. That short delay would not be injurious. In the meantime the freedmen would become more enlightened, and more fit to discharge the high duties of their new condition. In that time, too, the loyal Congress could mature their laws and so amend the Constitution as to secure the rights of every human being, and render disunion impossible. Heaven forbid that the southern States, or any one of them, should be represented on this floor until such muniments of freedom are built high and firm. Against our will they have been absent for four bloody years; against our will they must not come back until we are ready to receive them. Do not tell me that they are loyal representatives waiting for admission—until their States are loyal they can have no standing here. They would merely misrepresent their constituents.

I admit that this article is not as good as the one we sent to death in the Senate. In my judgment, we shall not approach the measure of justice until we have given every adult freedman a homestead on the land where he was born and toiled and suffered. Forty acres of land and a hut would be more valuable to him than the immediate right to vote. Unless we give them this we shall receive the censure of mankind and the curse of Heaven. That article referred to provided that if one of the injured race was excluded the State should forfeit the right to have any of them represented. That would have hastened their full enfranchisement. This section allows the States to discriminate among the same class, and receive proportionate credit in representation. This I dislike. But it is a short step forward. The large stride which we in vain proposed is dead; the murderers must answer to the suffering race. I would not have been the perpetrator. A load of misery must sit heavy on their souls.

The third section may encounter more difference of opinion here. Among the people I believe it will be the most popular of all the provisions; it prohibits rebels from voting for members of Congress and electors of President until 1870. My only objection to it is that it is too lenient. I know that there is a morbid sensibility, sometimes called mercy, which affects a few of all classes, from the priest to the clown, which has more sympathy for the murderer on the gallows than for his victim. I hope I have a heart as capable of feeling for human woe as others. I have long since wished that capital punishment were abolished. But I never dreamed that all punishment could be dispensed with in human society. Anarchy, treason, and violence would reign triumphant. Here is the mildest of all punishments ever inflicted on traitors. I might not consent to the extreme severity denounced upon them by a provisional Governor of Tennessee—I mean the late lamented Andrew Johnson of blessed memory—but I would have increased the severity of this section. I would be glad to see it extend to 1876, and to include all State and municipal as well as national elections. In my judgment we do not sufficiently protect the loyal men of the rebel States from the vindictive persecutions of their victorious rebel neighbors. Still I will move no amendment, nor vote for any, lest the whole fabric should tumble to pieces.

I need say nothing of the fourth section, for none dare object to it who is not himself a rebel. To the friend of justice, the friend of the Union, of the perpetuity of liberty, and the final triumph of the rights of man and their extension to every human being, let me say, sacrifice as we have done your peculiar views, and instead of vainly insisting upon the instantaneous operation of all that is right accept what is possible, and "all these things shall be added unto you."

ULYSSES S. GRANT, EIGHTEENTH PRESIDENT

By James Ford Rhodes

GRANT came as near being the unanimous choice of the country for President in 1868 as any candidate for that office ever has been. Besieged by both the Republican and Democratic parties to accept the nomination, his views were more in accord with the former, and in the race against Horatio Seymour, the Democratic candidate, Grant carried all but eight States.

Rhodes, from whose "History of the United States" this account is taken, by permission of the Macmillan Company, spent much time, during Grant's first administration, making industrial investigations in the South and gathering material for his monumental history, to the writing of which he devoted sixteen years. His narrative is impartial and sober, and is generally considered the best work covering the period treated.

BETWEEN the days of the two votes on the articles of impeachment the National Union Republican Convention assembled in Chicago [May 20] and with great enthusiasm nominated General Grant for President by a unanimous vote. Grant's position during the ante-Convention canvass had been an enviable one. Either party was willing to take him as its standard bearer. So far as he had ever had any political leanings they were Democratic. His only presidential vote had been cast for Buchanan and, had he acquired a residence in Illinois in 1860, he would have voted for Douglas. In 1867 the radical Republicans, fearing that Grant was not sound on Reconstruction and the negro, had desired the nomination of Chase; and there were also advocates of Colfax, who, as a great friend of his wrote, "has got the White House on the brain." Referring to Grant, Wade said, "A man may be all right on horses and all wrong on politics." But the shrewd Republican leaders and the bulk of the party wanted Grant and showed great eagerness to get him on their side. He had however told General Sherman that he would not accept a nomination for the Presidency. On August 9, John Sherman wrote: "If he has really made up his mind that he would like to hold that office he can have it. Popular opinion is all in his favor. . . . I see nothing in his way unless he is foolish enough to connect his future with the Democratic party." Yet, "if Grant declines then by all odds Chase is the safest man for the country." "So far as mortal ken can decide," wrote Bowles a month later, "Grant will take the game at a swoop." The Democratic victories of the autumn of 1867 convinced all the sagacious Republicans of influence that their success in 1868 would be in jeopardy if they could not bolster up their failing fortunes by the great personal popularity of Grant. Fate now intervened with Johnson's stupid quarrel which drove him avowedly into their fold. He was quick to acknowledge the situation and during the impeachment trial it became generally understood that he would accept the Republican nomination: he promptly confirmed expectation in a brief and characteristic letter of acceptance. . . .

Schuyler Colfax of Indiana, the Speaker of the House, was nominated for Vice-President on the fifth ballot, his most formidable competitor being Wade who led on every ballot until the last.

The important platform declarations were, the approval of the reconstruction policy of Congress, the denunciation as "a national crime" of all forms of repudiation and the demand that the debt of the nation be paid according to the spirit as well as the letter of the law.

The Democratic Convention was the more interesting owing to the maneuvers of George H. Pendleton and Chief Justice Chase, both Ohio men. . . .

That the Democrats were hopeful of success is shown by the eagerness with which their nomination was sought. And the enthusiasm engendered by their convention seemed to indicate that the country was weary of Republican rule. Pennsylvania, Ohio and Indiana held State elections in October and, to carry them, both sides made a strenuous effort; in Pennsylvania and Indiana it was a sharp contest. Pennsylvania went Republican by less than ten thousand; and Hendricks, who had accepted the Democratic nomination for Governor of Indiana in the hope of carrying the State, so that he might be reëlected Senator, was beaten by only 961. Ohio, a more certain Republican State than either, gave the Republican candidate only 17,000 majority. These elections, however, made the main result a practically foregone conclusion. Seymour with great energy took the stump and made a number of excellent and moderate speeches in Western New York, Ohio, Indiana, Illinois and Pennsylvania; but the tide had set against his party and his efforts to stem it were ineffectual. Grant carried 26 States receiving 214 electoral votes while Seymour had a majority in 8 that chose 80 electors. Of the late Confederate States, North Carolina, South Carolina, Florida, Alabama, Arkansas and Tennessee went for Grant; Georgia and Louisiana for Seymour. Virginia, Mississippi and Texas were, as we have seen, unreconstructed and took no part in the presidential election. The victory for Grant was not so overwhelming as the figures seem to indicate. Seymour carried New York, New Jersey and Oregon and had he received as well the votes of the "solid South," which were a possession of the Democrats from 1880 to 1892, he would have been elected. It was however believed by Republicans at the North that Georgia and Louisiana had been carried for Seymour by "organized assassination" and that in Louisiana fraud had come to the assistance of terror.

The strongest factor in Republican success was the immense personal popularity of Grant; the adroit use made of the unrest and "outrages" at the South was another. That the result did not turn on the financial question is obvious enough; for New York and New Jersey, hard money States, went for Seymour while Ohio and Indiana where the "Ohio idea" was most influential went for Grant. Could Seymour have made his own platform and chosen his associate on the ticket, the election would have been more closely contested but no combination of circumstances could have beaten Grant. His candidacy allayed the discontent both with negro suffrage and with the high-handed rule at the South. And the result of his election was generally tranquillizing. . . .

Amid the general acclamations of the people on March 4, 1869 General Grant was inaugurated President. No President since Washington, except Monroe and Lincoln at their second inaugurations, went into office so favorably regarded by men of all parties. As I have previously stated, he could have had the Democratic nomination had he not decided to cast his lot with the Republicans; and although the contest had been a lively one, Democratic zeal had in hardly any degree been directed against Grant but rather against Republican policy. Thus Democrats regarded him as their President as well as that of the party which chose him. His record as a general had won the admiration, and his simple and honest nature the affections, of the educated and highly placed as well as of the plain people. In the ceremony of inauguration there was but one jarring note. Grant felt so bitterly towards Johnson, because of their controversy of the year before, that he departed from the usual custom and declined to drive with him in the same carriage from the White House to the Capitol.

His brief inaugural address was characteristic. "The responsibilities of the position I feel," he said, "but accept them without fear. The office has come to me unsought; I commence its duties untrammeled." He had a great opportunity; only Washington's and Lincoln's were greater. In his appointments for the Cabinet he showed his complete independence, choosing his ministers without the usual consultations with prominent men of the party and without regard to public sentiment and its canvassing of the merits of different candidates through the press. Hardly any newspaper guessing of the make-up of the Cabinet was even in part correct and five of the appointments were a general surprise, some of them indeed to the men themselves who were named. Elihu B. Washburne of Illinois, the faithful friend of Lincoln and Grant, was nominated for Secretary of State. He had been an excellent representative in Congress but was entirely without fitness for the State Department. For Secretary of the Treasury the President's choice fell upon Alexander T. Stewart, the rich and successful dry goods merchant of New York City. Some senators and representatives did not like this selection but it was well received by the public. Stewart was one of the three richest men in the country and had built up his immense fortune from a small inheritance by remarkably able business management. For a number of years the newspapers had been full of anecdotes of his executive ability as shown in his systematization of a large trade and his excellent choice of subordinates; and few men outside of public life were better known. Grant, so it was said, had observed the skill with which Stewart conducted his

ULYSSES S. GRANT

private affairs and desired to enlist it in the public service. His nomination, along with all the others, was promptly and unanimously confirmed, but within two days it was discovered that he was not eligible for the office. The Act of September 2, 1789 establishing the Department provided that no one appointed Secretary of the Treasury should "directly or indirectly be concerned or interested in carrying on the business of trade or commerce." The President asked Congress to exempt Stewart by joint resolution from the operation of the act and Sherman asked unanimous consent of the Senate to introduce a bill repealing so much of the act as made Stewart ineligible, his intention being to have it passed at once; but Sumner objected to such a summary proceeding. The President withdrew his request, and, "to fill a vacancy," appointed George S. Boutwell of Massachusetts, a sturdy Puritan and politician of sterling virtue but with no especial qualifications for Secretaryship of the Treasury. . . . Jacob D. Cox, of Ohio, was made Secretary of the Interior; E. Rockwood Hoar, of Massachusetts, Attorney-General; John A. Rawlins, Grant's faithful friend and mentor in the army, was appointed Secretary of War, and John A. J. Creswell, of Maryland, Postmaster-General.

BLACK FRIDAY

By J. K. Medbery

THE name, Black Friday, is applied to the first of two disastrous days (September 24-5, 1869) in the financial history of the United States. It involved a panic caused by the effort of Gould and Fisk to corner the gold market, and originated in a fight between them and the Vanderbilts for control of the Erie Railroad. A campaign of bribery and corruption was carried on that soiled the reputations of public officials, including legislatures and judges by wholesale, reaching its climax in the gold conspiracy of 1869 and Black Friday. An attempt was made to control President Grant himself.

The event was a sort of precursor to a subsequent evil experience Grant had in Wall Street, after his second term as President, when he became a partner in the firm of Grant and Ward, which came to grief and involved him in financial ruin. This contemporaneous account is given in Medbery's "Men and Mysteries of Wall Street."

ON the 22d of September gold stood at 137½ when Trinity bells rung out the hour of twelve. By two it was at 139. Before night its lowest quotation was 141. This ascent, regular, unfluctuating, and evidently predetermined, carried the more alarm by the very extent of the rise. In the old Rebellion days a ten-per-cent increase in eight hours was an affair of no moment whatever. It happened every week, sometimes twice and thrice a week. But since the sharp vibrations of June 16 and 18, 1866, when gold rose and fell from 154 to 160, and again from 133 to 167¾, the utmost daily range had been two per cent, with occasional fractional additions. Three years of dull monotony, and now an advance of three and a half per cent in five hours! At the same time the Stock Market conditions exhibited tokens of excessive febrility, New York Central dropping twenty-three per cent and Harlem thirteen. Loans had become extremely difficult to negotiate. The most usurious prices for a twenty-four hours' turn were freely paid. The storm was palpably reaching the proportions of a tempest.

Nevertheless, the brokers on the bear side strove manfully under their burden. The character and purposes of the clique were fully known. Whatever of mystery had heretofore enfolded them was now boldly thrown aside, and the men of Erie, with the sublime Fisk in the forefront of the assailing column, assured the shorts that they could not settle too quickly, since it remained with the ring, now holding calls for one hundred millions, either to kindly compromise at 150 or to carry the metal to 200 and nail it there. This threat was accompanied by consequences in which the mailed hand revealed itself under the silken glove. The movement had intertwisted itself deep into the affairs of every dealer in the Street, and entangled in its meshes vast numbers of outside speculators. In borrowing or in margins the entire capital of the former had been nearly absorbed, while some five millions had been deposited by the latter with their brokers in answer to repeated calls. When Thursday morning rose, gold started at $141\frac{5}{8}$, and soon shot up to 144. Then the clique began to tighten the screws. The shorts received peremptory orders to increase their borrowing margins. At the same moment the terms of loans overnight were raised beyond the pitch of ordinary human endurance. Stories were insidiously circulated exciting suspicion of the integrity of the Administration, and strengthening the belief that the National Treasury would bring no help to the wounded bears. Whispers of an impending lock-up of money were prevalent; and the fact, then shrewdly suspected, and now known, of certifications of checks to the amount of twenty-five millions by one bank alone on that day lent color to the rumor. Many brokers lost courage, and settled instantly. The Gold Boom shook with the conflict, and the battle prolonged itself into a midnight session at the Fifth Avenue Hotel. The din of the tumult had penetrated to the upper chambers of journalism. Reporters were on the alert. The great dailies magnified the struggle, and the Associated Press spread intelligence of the excitement to remote sections.

When Friday opened clear and calm, the pavement of Broad and New Streets soon filled up with unwonted visitors. All the idle population of the city and its neighborhood crowded into the financial quarter to witness the throes of the tortured shorts. Blended with the merely curious were hundreds of outside speculators who had ventured their all in the great stake, and trembled in doubt of the honor of their dealers. Long before 9 A. M. these men, intensely interested in the day's encounter, poured through the alleyway from Broad Street, and between the narrow walls of New Street, surging up around the doorways, and piling themselves densely and painfully within the cramped galleries of the Room itself. They had made good the fresh calls for margins up to 143, the closing figure of the night before. The paramount question now was, How would gold open? They had not many minutes to wait. Pressing up to the fountain, around which some fifty brokers had already congregated, a bull operator with resonant voice bid 145 for twenty thousand. The shout startled the galleries. Their margins were once more in jeopardy. Would their brokers remain firm? It was a terrible moment. The bears closed round the aggressors. Yells and shrieks filled the air. A confused and baffling whirl of sounds ensued, in which all sorts of fractional bids and offers mingled, till '46 emerged from the chaos. The crowd within the arena increased rapidly in numbers. The clique agents became vociferous. Gold steadily pushed forward in its perilous upward movement from '46 to '47, thence to '49, and, pausing for a brief twenty minutes, dashed on to 150½. It was now considerably past the hour of regular session. The President was in the chair. The Secretary's pen was bounding over his registry book. The floor of the Gold Room was covered with three hundred agitated dealers and operators, shouting, heaving in masses against and around the iron railing of the fountain, falling back upon the approaches of the committee-rooms and the outer entrance, guarded with rigorous care by sturdy doorkeepers. Many of the principal brokers of the street were there,—Kimber, who had turned traitor to the ring; Colgate, the Baptist; Clews, a veteran government broker; one of the Marvins; James Brown; Albert Speyer, and dozens of others hardly less famous. Every individual of all that seething throng had a personal stake beyond, and, in natural human estimate, a thousandfold more dear than that of any outside patron, no matter how deeply or ruinously that patron might be involved. At 11 of the dial gold was $150\frac{1}{2}$; in six minutes it jumped to 155. Then the pent-up tiger spirit burst from control. The arena rocked as the Coliseum may have rocked when the gates of the wild beasts were thrown open, and with wails and shrieks the captives of the empire sprang to merciless encounter with the ravenous demons of the desert. The storm of voices lost human semblance. Clenched hands, livid faces, pallid foreheads on which beads of cold sweat told of the interior anguish, lurid, passion-fired eyes,—all the symptoms of a fever which at any moment might become frenzy were there. The shouts of golden millions upon millions hurtled in all ears. The labor of years was disappearing and reappearing in the wave line of advancing and receding prices. With fortunes melting away in a second, with five hundred millions of gold in process of sale or purchase, with the terror of yet higher prices, and the exultation which came and went with the whispers of fresh men entering from Broad Street bearing confused rumors of the probable interposition of the government, it is not hard to understand how reason faltered on its throne, and operators became reckless, buying or selling without thought of the morrow or consciousness of the present.

Then came the terrific bid of Albert Speyer for any number of millions at 160. William Parks sold instantly two millions and a half in one lot. Yet the bids so far from yielding rose to 161, 162, 162½. For five minutes the Board reeled under the ferocity of the attack. Seconds became hours. The agony of Wellington awaiting Blücher was in the souls of the bears. Then a broker, reported to be acting for Baring and Brothers at London, sold five millions to the clique at the top price of the day. Hallgarten followed; and as the shorts were gathering courage, the certain news that the Secretary of the Treasury had come to the rescue swept through the chamber, gold fell from 160 to 140, and thence, with hardly the interval of one quotation, to 133. The end had come, and the exhausted operators streamed out of the stifling hall into the fresh air of the street. To them, however, came no peace. In some offices customers by dozens, whose margins were irrevocably burnt away in the smelting-furnaces of the Gold Board, confronted their dealers with taunts and threats of violence for their treachery. In others the nucleus of mobs began to form, and, as the day wore off, Broad Street had the aspect of a riot. Huge masses of men gathered before the doorway of Smith, Gould, Martin & Co. and Heath & Co. Fisk was assaulted, and his life threatened. Deputy-sheriffs and police-officers appeared on the scene. In Brooklyn a company of troops were held in readiness to march upon Wall Street.

When night came, Broad Street and its vicinity saw an unwonted sight. The silence and the darkness; whichever rests over the lower city after seven of the evening, was broken by the blaze of gas-light from a hundred windows, and the footfall of clerks hurrying from a hasty repast back to their desks. Until long after Trinity bells pealed out the dawn of a new day, men bent over their books, scrutinized the Clearing-House statement for the morrow, took what thought was possible for the future. At the Gold Exchange Bank the weary accountants were making ineffective efforts to complete Thursday's business. That toilful midnight, at the close of the last great passion-day of the bullion-worshipers, will be ever memorable for its anxieties and unsatisfying anguish.

Saturday brought no relief. The Gold Board met only to adjourn, as the Clearing-House had been incapable of the task of settling its accounts, complicated as they were by ever fresh failures. The small brokers had gone under by scores. The rumors of the impending suspension of some of the largest houses of the Street gave fresh grounds for fear. The Stock Exchange was now the center of attraction. If that yielded, all was lost. To sustain the market was vital. But whence was the saving power to come? All through yesterday shares had been falling headlong. New York Central careened to 148, and then recovered to 185¾. Hudson plunged from 173 to 145. Pittsburgh fell to 68. Northwest reached 62½. The shrinkage throughout all securities had been not less than thirty millions. Would the impulse downward continue? The throngs which filled the corridors and overhung the stairway from which one can look down upon the Long Room saw only mad tumult, heard only the roar of the biddings. For any certain knowledge they might have been in Alaska. But the financial public in the quiet of their offices, and nervously scrutinizing the prices reeled off from the automaton telegraph, saw that Vanderbilt was supporting the New York stocks, and that the weakness in other shares was not sufficient to shadow forth panic. It soon became known that the capitalists from Philadelphia, Boston, and the great Western cities had thrown themselves into the breach, and were earning fortunes for themselves as well as gratitude from the money-market, by the judicious daring of their purchases. The consciousness of this new element was quieting, but Wall Street was still too feverish to be reposed by any ordinary anodyne. A run on the Tenth National Bank had commenced, and all day long a steady line of dealers filed up to the counter of the paying teller demanding their balances. The courage and the ability in withstanding the attack which were shown by the president and his associates deserve something more than praise. The Gold Exchange Bank witnessed a similar scene, angry brokers assaulting the clerks and threatening all possible things unless instantaneous settlements were made. The freedom with which the press had given details of the explosion had been extremely hurtful to the credit of many of the best houses. In a crisis like that of Black Friday the sluicegates of passion open. Cloaked in the masquerade of genuine distrust, came forth whispers whose only origin was in ancient enmities, long-treasured spites, the soundless depths of unquenchable malignities. Firms of stanchest reputation felt the rapier stroke of old angers. The knowledge that certain houses were large holders of particular stocks was the signal of attacks upon the shares. Despite of outside orders for vast amounts, these influences had their effect upon securities, and aided to tighten the loan market. One, one and a half, two and even four per cent were the compulsory terms on which money could alone be borrowed to carry stocks over Sunday.

On Monday the 27th the Gold Board met, but only to be informed that the Clearing-House was not yet ready to complete the work of Friday. Important accounts had been kept back, and the dealings, swollen in sum-total to five hundred millions, were beyond the capacity of the clerical force of the Gold Bank to grapple with. A resolution was brought forward proposing the resumption of operations Ex-Clearing House. The measure took the members by surprise, for a moment quivered between acceptance and rejection, and then was swiftly tabled. It was an immense bear scheme, for no Exchange can transact business where its dealers are under suspicion. All outstanding accounts require immediate fulfilment. Failure to make good deliveries would have insured the instant selling out of defaulters "under the rule." As the majority of brokers were inextricably involved in the late difficulty, the only consequence would have been to throw them into bankruptcy, thus bringing some sixty millions under the hammer. The market could not have borne up under such an avalanche. It was decided that the Room should be kept open for borrowings and loans, but that all dealings should be suspended. One result of this complication was that gold had no fixed value. It could be bought at one house for 133, and at other offices sold for 139. The Board thus proved its utility at the very juncture when least in favor.

The remaining history of the panic need not long detain us. As more and more light fell upon the tactics of the ring, it was seen that the final basis of their scheme was the use of a very old trick, first put in practice long ago on the London Stock Exchange. Two dealers league together. One buys all that he can by cash or credit; the other sells proportionately. One loses heavily; the other gains vastly. The former breaks and retires; the latter remains, and secretly divides up the profits. With proper regard for that bulwark of the American people, the libel law, we shall not undertake to carry out the comparison. It may not be unfair, however, to note as an example of the proportions of the struggle, that Albert Speyer, on Friday, bought $47,000,000 and failed to make good his contracts; while Belden & Co. "broke" for $50,000,000; and several others, supposed to be acting for the clique, had obligations out for so many millions that no attempt has yet been made to give them numerical computation.

THE FIRST TRANSCONTINENTAL RAILROAD

By John P. Davis

ON May 10, 1869, the last spike was driven, at Promontory Point, Utah, that joined the Union and Central Pacific and signalized the completion of the first transcontinental American railroad. In "The Union Pacific Railway," from which this account is taken by permission of the Scott, Forsman Company, the author tells of the ingenious plans to apprise the country of the "wedding of the rails."

Spikes of gold were contributed by California and neighboring Territories. A silver sledge was provided and wires were connected with it so that the sound of each stroke, delivered alternately by President Stanford, of the Central Pacific, and Vice-President Durant, of the Union Pacific, was instantaneously transmitted to a nation-wide audience. Locomotives were drawn up to "touch noses," bands blared, there was feasting in private cars, and a parade of banners reading, "What God hath joined together let no man put asunder."

THE inducements offered by the Act of 1862 were insufficient to attract to the Union Pacific individual capitalists desirous to display industrial heroism and save the nation, but doubling the amount of the prizes by the amendments of 1864 had the desired effect, and a beginning was made by the completion of eleven miles of the Union Pacific by September 25, 1865, and of forty miles by the end of that year. On October 5, 1866, the mileage had increased to two hundred forty-seven. By January 1, 1867, the road was finished and operated to a point three hundred five miles west from Omaha. In 1867 two hundred forty miles were built. The year 1868 produced four hundred twenty-five miles; and the first four months of 1869 added the one hundred twenty-five miles necessary to complete the road to its junction with the Central Pacific at Promontory Point.

Work on the Central Pacific had begun at Sacramento more than a year before it was begun on the Union Pacific at Omaha; and by the time the first eleven miles of the latter had been completed, the former had attained a length of fifty-six miles, increased by January 1, 1867, to ninety-four miles. In 1867 forty-six miles were built; in 1868 three hundred sixty-three miles were added; in 1869 the remaining one hundred eighty-six miles were covered, and Promontory Point was reached. The Union Pacific had built one thousand eighty-six miles from Omaha; the Central Pacific had built six hundred eighty-nine miles from Sacramento.

The natural obstacles presented by the mountains and desert land, the absence of timber on the prairies, of water in the mountains, and of both in the alkali desert, had made the work exceptionally difficult and expensive. The Central Pacific, though under the necessity of getting its iron, finished supplies, and machinery by sea, via Cape Horn or Panama, had the advantage of Chinese coolie labor and the unified management of its construction company; while the Union Pacific, having no railway connection until January, 1867, was subjected to the hardship of getting its supplies overland from the termini of the Iowa railways or by the Missouri River boats, and had to depend on intractable Irish labor and the warring factions of the Crédit Mobilier.

The Sierra Nevada furnished the Central Pacific all the timber needed for ties, trestlework and snowsheds, but the Union Pacific had little or no timber along its line, except the unserviceable cottonwood of the Platte Valley, and many boats were kept busy for a hundred miles above and below Omaha on the Missouri River in furnishing ties and heavy timbers. Both roads were being built through a new, uninhabited, and uncultivated region, where were no foundries, machine-shops, or any other conveniences of a settled country. The large engine used in the Union Pacific Railway shops was dragged across the country to Omaha from Des Moines. Twenty-five thousand men, about equally divided between two companies, are said to have been employed during the closing months of the great work. Several thousand Chinamen had been imported to California for the express purpose of building the Central Pacific. On the Union Pacific, European emigrant labor, principally Irish, was employed. At the close of the Civil War many of the soldiers, laborers, teamsters and camp-followers drifted west to gather the aftermath of the war in the work of railway construction.

The work was essentially military, and one is not surprised to find among the superintendents and managers a liberal sprinkling of military titles. The surveying parties were always accompanied by a detachment of soldiery as a protection against interference by Indians. The construction-trains were amply supplied with rifles and other arms, and it was boasted that a gang of tracklayers could be transmuted at any moment into a battalion of infantry. . . .

The only settlements between Omaha and Sacramento in 1862 were those of the Mormons in Utah, and Denver and a few mining camps in Colorado and Nevada. Colorado was given over to the Kansas Pacific, and Salt Lake City was left for a branch line; Ogden, a Mormon town of a few hundred inhabitants, was the only station between the termini of the Union Central Pacific. The necessities of the work of construction created new settlements and stations as it progressed, and as fast as the road was completed to each convenient point it was operated to it, while the work went on from the terminus town as a headquarters or base of operations; thus, when the entire line was put in operation, July 15, 1869, such places as North Platte, Kearney, and Cheyenne had "got a start," while other towns, being made the termini of branch lines, secured the additional impulse due in general to junction towns. Some of the "headquarters towns," like Benton, enjoyed only a temporary, Jonah's gourd existence, and nothing is now left to mark their former location. The life in them was rough and profligate in the extreme. . . .

It had been expected that the Central Pacific, chartered by the State of California, would build east to the Nevada boundary, and that the Union Pacific, chartered by the National Government, would build westward from Omaha through the territories to a meeting at the California boundary. But the object of the Pacific Railroad charter was to secure a railway from the Missouri to the Pacific, by whomsoever constructed, and its terms (section 10 of the Act of 1862) had provided that "in case said first-named [Union Pacific] company shall complete their line to the eastern boundary of California before it is completed across said State by the Central Pacific Railroad Company of California, said first-named company is hereby authorized to continue in constructing the same through California until said roads shall meet and connect, and the Central Pacific Railroad Company of California, after completing its road across said State, is authorized to continue the construction of said railroad and telegraph through the Territories of the United States to the Missouri River, including the branch lines specified, until said roads shall meet and connect."

This was changed in the Act of 1864 (section 16) to a provision that the Central Pacific might "extend their line of road eastward one hundred fifty miles on the established route, so as to meet and connect with the line of the Union Pacific road." Of which change Collis P. Huntington, of the Central Pacific, has said: " 'One hundred fifty miles' should not have gone into the bill; but I said to Mr. Union Pacific, when I saw it, I would take that out as soon as I wanted it out. In 1866 I went to Washington. I got a large majority of them without the use of a dollar." Accordingly the

Act of 1866 renewed the original provision of the Act of 1862, and provided (section 2) that "the Central Pacific Railroad Company of California, with the consent and approval of the Secretary of the Interior, are hereby authorized to locate, construct, and continue their road eastward in a continuous completed line, until they shall meet and connect with the Union Pacific Railroad."

The renewed provision resulted in the greatest race on record. The Central Pacific had to surmount the Sierra Nevada range at the beginning of its course, but the "Big Four," under the legal disguise of Charles Crocker and Company, were plucky, and the rise of seven thousand twelve feet above the sea-level in the one hundred five miles east of Sacramento to Summit was accomplished by the autumn of 1867. The Central Pacific did not wait for the completion of its fourteen tunnels, and especially its longest one of more than one thousand six hundred feet, at Summit, but hauled iron and supplies, and even locomotives, over the Sierra Nevada beyond the completed track, and went ahead with track-laying, to be connected later with the track through the tunnels. The Union Pacific had comparatively easy work from Omaha along the Platte Valley and up the slope to the summit of the Rocky Mountains, and boasted that its line would reach the eastern side of the Sierra Nevada before the Central Pacific had surmounted it. But the boast was not warranted.

In the autumn of 1867 the invading army of Mongolians emerged from the mountains on the west, while the rival army of Celts had reached the summit of the Black Hills and were beginning their descent into the Great Basin on the east. Every mile now meant a prize of $64,000 to $96,000 for the contending giants, with the commercial advantage of the control of the traffic of the Salt Lake Valley in addition. The construction of road went on at the rate of four to ten miles a day. Each of the two companies had more than ten thousand men at work.

For the purpose of facilitating the work, the amendatory Act of 1864 had permitted, on the certificate of the chief engineer and government commissioners, that a portion of the work required to prepare the road for the superstructure was done, that a proportion of the bonds to be fully earned on the final completion of the work, not exceeding two-thirds of the value of the portion of the work done, and not exceeding two-thirds of the whole amount of bonds to be earned, should be delivered to each company; the full benefit of this inducement was sought by each of the contestants. The Union Pacific Company had its parties of graders working two hundred miles in advance of its completed line in places as far west as Humboldt Wells, but financial difficulties prevented its following up this advantage. The Central Pacific Company, on the other hand, had its grading-parties one hundred miles ahead of its completed line and thirty miles east of Ogden.

94 FIRST TRANSCONTINENTAL RAILROAD

When the two roads met at Promontory Point, it was found that the Central Pacific had graded eighty miles to the east that it never would cover, and the Union Pacific had wasted a million dollars on grading west of the meeting-place that it could not use. The Central Pacific had obtained from the Secretary of the Treasury an advance of two-thirds of the bond subsidy on its graded line to Echo Summit, about forty miles east of Ogden, before its completed line had reached Promontory Point; while the Union Pacific had actually laid its track to and westward from Ogden, and appeared thus to have gained the advantage of controlling the Salt Lake Valley traffic from Ogden as a base.

The Union Pacific was pushing westward from Ogden with its completed line about a mile distant from and parallel with the surveyed and graded line of the Central Pacific, and the two companies were each claiming the right to build the line between Ogden and Promontory Point on their separate surveys. The completed lines were threatening to lap as the graded lines already lapped, when Congress interfered and tried to clear the muddle by statute. Before Congress could reach a conclusion, the companies compromised their differences, and Congress then approved the settlement by a joint resolution, April 10, 1869, "That the common terminus of the Union Pacific and the Central Pacific railroads shall be at or near Ogden; and the Union Pacific Railroad Company shall build, and the Central Pacific Railroad

FIRST TRANSCONTINENTAL RAILROAD 95

Company pay for and own, the railroad from the terminus aforesaid to Promontory Summit, at which point the rails shall meet and connect and form one continuous line." In the following year Congress, by further enactment, fixed "the common terminus and point of junction" at a particular point about five miles "northwest of the station at Ogden"; later the Union Pacific leased to the Central Pacific the five miles of track between the station at Ogden and the point fixed by Congress; thus Ogden became the actual point of junction of the two links of the completed Pacific Railway. . . .

The disputed question of the point of junction did not interfere with a due celebration of the meeting and joining of the two "ends of track" at Promontory Point on May 10, 1869. A space of about one hundred feet was left between the ends of the lines. Early in the day, Leland Stanford, Governor of California and president of the Central Pacific, arrived with his party from the west; in the forenoon Vice-President Durant and Directors Duff and Dillon, of the Union Pacific, with other men, including a delegation of Mormon "saints" from Salt Lake City, came in on a train from the east. The National Government was represented by a detachment of regulars from Fort Douglas, with the opportune accessories of ornamental officers and a military band. Curious Mexicans, Indians and half-breeds, with the Chinese, negro and Irish laborers, lent to the auspicious little gathering a suggestive air of cosmopolitanism. The ties were laid for the rails in the open space, and while the coolies from the West laid the rails at one end, the Irishmen from the East laid them at the other end, until they met and joined.

The last spike remained to be driven. Telegraphic wires were so connected that each blow of the sledge could be reported instantly on the telegraphic instruments in most of the large cities from the Atlantic to the Pacific; corresponding blows were struck on the bell of the City Hall in San Francisco, and with the last blow of the sledge a cannon was fired at Fort Point. General Safford presented a spike of gold, silver and iron as the offering of the Territory of Arizona; Tuttle, of Nevada, performed with a spike of silver a like office for his State. The tie of California laurel was put in place, and Doctor Harkness, of California, presented the last spike of gold in behalf of his State. A silver sledge had also been presented for the occasion. The driving of the spike by President Stanford and Vice-President Durant was greeted with lusty cheers; and the shouts of the six hundred persons present, to the accompaniment of the screams of the locomotive whistles and the blare of the military band, in the midst of the desert, found hearty and enthusiastic echoes in the great cities east and west.

THE OVERTHROW OF THE TWEED RING

By E. Benjamin Andrews

D*R. ANDREWS, from whose "History of the Last Quarter-Century of the United States, 1870-1895," this account is taken, by permission of Charles Scribner's Sons, graduated from Brown University the year (1870) that the plundering operations of the notorious Tweed Ring in New York were exposed. Later he was president of that university, was superintendent of schools in Chicago and became chancellor of the University of Nebraska.*

As Dr. Andrews relates, it was in 1872, following a vigorous investigation and prosecution conducted by a committee of seventy citizens of New York, headed by Samuel J. Tilden, that "Boss" Tweed was indicted for forgery and grand larceny. He boasted of having amassed a fortune of $20,000,000. He was tried, convicted and imprisoned. Released on a technicality, he was rearrested, jailed, escaped to Spain, was brought back and again lodged in prison until April 12, 1878, when he died.

IN the summer of 1870 proof was published of vast frauds by leading [New York] city officials, prominent among them "Boss" William M. Tweed, who, in the language of Judge Noah Davis, "saw fit to pervert the powers with which he was clothed, in a manner more infamous, more outrageous, than any instance of a like character which the history of the civilized world afforded."

William Marcy Tweed was born in 1823, at 24 Cherry Street, New York City. A youth devoted to business made him a fair penman and an adept reckoner, but not a business man. He, indeed, once attempted business, but, as he gave his chief attention to speculation, gambling and ward politics, completely failed, so that he seems

forever to have renounced legitimate money-making.
As a volunteer fireman, known as "Big Six," a gross,
licentious Falstaff of real life, albeit loyal and helpful
to his friends, Tweed led the "Roughs," being opposed
by his more decent fellows, the "Quills." The tide of
"respectability," receding uptown, left Tweed's ward
in the hands of poor immigrants or the sons of such,
who became partly his willing accomplices, partly his
unwitting tools, in his onslaughts upon taxpayers. He
began these forays at twenty-seven, as Alderman, suspended them for a time in Congress, resumed them in
1857 as Public School Commissioner, continued and
enlarged them as member and four times president of
the Board of Supervisors, and brought them to a climax as a functionary of the Street Department. He
thus became, in time, the central sun in the system of
brilliant luminaries known as the "Tweed Ring."

The multitudinous officials of the city were the
Ring's slaves. At one time eight hundred policemen
stood guard to prevent a hostile majority in Tammany
Hall itself from meeting. The thugs of the city, nicknamed "Tweed's lambs," rendered invaluable services
at caucus and convention. Two days before election
these venal cohorts would assemble in the 340 election
districts, each man of them being listed and registered
under several assumed names and addresses. From
Tweed's house in 1868 six registered, from Justice
Shandley's nine, from the Coroner's thirteen. A State
Senator's house was put down as the home of thirty
voters. One Alderman's residence nominally housed

twenty, another's twenty-five, an Assemblyman's fifteen. And so it went. Bales of fictitious naturalization papers were secured. One year 105,000 blank applications and 69,000 certificates were ordered printed. In one case thirteen men, in another fifteen, were naturalized in five minutes. The new citizens "put in" election day following their leaders from polling-place to polling-place as needed.

When thieves could be kept in power by such means plunder was easy and brazen. Contractors on public works were systematically forced to pay handsome bonuses to the Ring. One of them testified "When I commenced building I asked Tweed how to make out the bills, and he said, 'Have fifteen per cent. over.' I asked what that was for, and he said, 'Give that to me and I will take care of your bills.' I handed him the percentage after that." Innumerable methods of fraud were successfully tried. During the year 1863 the expenditures of the Street Department were $650,000. Within four years Tweed quadrupled them. A species of asphalt paving, dubbed "Fisk's poultice," so bad that a grand jury actually declared it a public nuisance, was laid in great quantities at vast cost to the city. Official advertising was doled to twenty-six daily and fifty-four weekly sheets, of which twenty-seven vanished on its withdrawal. But all the other robber enterprises paled before the city Court House job. This structure, commenced in 1868, under stipulation that it should not cost more than $250,000, was in 1871 still unfinished after an outlay of $8,000,000, four times as much as was spent on Parliament House in London. Its ostensible cost, at least, was not less than $12,000,000. As by witchcraft the city's debt was in two years more than doubled. The Ring's operations cheated the city's taxpayers, first and last, out of no less than $160,000,000, "or four times the fine levied on Paris by the German army." Though wallowing in lucre, and prodigal withal, Tweed was yet insatiably greedy. "His hands were everywhere, and everywhere they were feeling for money." In 1871 he boasted of being worth $20,000,000, and vowed soon to be as rich as Vanderbilt.

With his coarse nature the Boss reveled in jibes made at the expense of his honor. He used gleefully to show his friends the safe where he kept money for bribing legislators, finding those of the "Tammany Republican" stripe easiest game. Of the contractor who was decorating his country place at Greenwich he inquired, pointing to a statue, "Who the hell is that?" "That is Mercury, the god of merchants and thieves," was the reply. "That's bully!" said Tweed. "Put him over the front door." His donation of $100 for an altar cloth in the Greenwich Methodist Church the trustees sent back, declaring that they wanted none of his stolen money. Other charitable gifts of his were better received.

The city papers, even those least corruptible, were for long either neutral or else favorable to the Ring, but its doings were by no means unknown. They were matters of general surmise and criticism, criticism that seemed hopeless, so hard was it to obtain exact evidence.

But pride goeth before a fall. Amid its greatest triumph the Ring sowed the wind whence rose the whirlwind which wrought its ruin. At a secret meeting held in the house of John Morrissey, pugilist member of Congress, certain of the unsatisfied, soon known as the "Young Democracy," planned a revolt. Endeavoring to prevent the grant by the New York Legislature of a new charter which the Ring sought, the insurgents met apparent defeat, which, however, ultimately proved victory, Tweed building for himself far worse than he knew. The new charter, abstractly good, in concentrating power concentrated responsibility also, showing the outraged people, when awakened, where to strike for liberty. In spite of whitewashing by prominent citizens, of blandishments and bulldozing, of attempts to buy the stock of the "Times" and to boycott "Harper's Weekly" where Nast's cartoons—his first work of the kind—gave the Ring international notoriety, the reform spirit proved irresistible. The bar had been servile or quiet, but the New York Bar Association was now formed, which at once became what it has ever since been, a most influential censor of the bench. The Young Democracy grew powerful. Public-spirited citizens organized a Council of Political Reform.

The occasion of conclusive exposure was trivial enough. Sheriff O'Brien was refused part of what he thought his share of the sheriff fees. An expert accountant in the Comptroller's office supplied him with damning evidence against the Ring. On July 18, 1871, Mr. O'Brien walked into the "Times" office and, handing the editor a bundle of documents, said, "There are all the figures; you can do with them just what you please." The figures were published on the 20th in an exhibit printed in English and German, causing excitement compared with which that arising from the Orange Riot of July 12th seemed trifling. The sensation did not end with talk. On September 4th a mass-meeting of citizens was held at Cooper Institute and a committee of seventy prominent men chosen to probe the frauds and to punish the perpetrators. For the work of prosecution the Attorney-General appointed Charles O'Conor, who associated with himself the ablest counsel. Samuel J. Tilden was conspicuously active in the prosecution, thus laying the foundation for that popularity which made him the Governor of New York, 1875-'77, and in 1876 the Democratic candidate for the Presidency of the United States.

On October 28, 1871, Tweed was arrested and gave a million dollars' bail. In November, the same year, he was elected to the State Senate, but did not take his seat. On December 16th he was again arrested, and released on $5,000 bail. The jury disagreed on the first suit, but on the second he was convicted and sentenced to pay a fine of $12,500 and to suffer twelve years' imprisonment. This sentence was set aside by the Court of Appeals and Tweed's discharge ordered. In the meantime other suits had been brought, among them, one to recover $6,000,-000. Failing to find bail for $3,000,000, he was sent to the Ludlow Street Jail. Being allowed to ride in the Park and occasionally to visit his residence, one day in December he escaped from his keepers. After hiding for several months he succeeded in reaching Cuba.

A fisherman found him, sunburnt and weary but not homesick, and led him to Santiago. Instead of taking him to a hotel, Tweed's guide handed him over to the police as probably some American filibuster come to free Cuba. The American consul procured his release (his passports had been given him under an assumed name), but later found him out. The discovery was too late, for he had again escaped and embarked for Spain, thinking there to be at rest, as we then had no extradition treaty with that country. Landing at Vigo, he found the governor of the place with police waiting for him, and was soon homeward bound on an American war-vessel. Caleb Cushing, our Minister at Madrid, had learned of his departure for that realm, and had put the authorities on their guard. To help them identify their man he furnished them a caricature by Nast, representing Tweed as a Tammany policeman gripping two boys by the hair. Thus it came about that "Twid antelme" was apprehended by our peninsular friends as a child-stealer. Though everything possible was done to render him comfortable in jail, Tweed sighed for liberty. He promised, if released, to turn State's evidence and to give up all his property and effects. Some papers suggested that the public pitied the man and would be glad to have him set free. No compromise with him was made, however, and he continued in jail till his death in 1878.

THE FIFTEENTH AMENDMENT

By Senator Henry Wilson

THIS amendment, adopted in 1870, gave the American negro his full civil rights, as a sequel to the thirteenth amendment, of 1865, which legally destroyed the institution of slavery. Accompanying the text of the amendment is the main part of a speech which Wilson, the "Natick Cobbler," delivered in the United States Senate at the time of its adoption.

Wilson had succeeded Edward Everett as Senator from Massachusetts in 1855, and retained his seat until 1873. Before the Civil War he was one of the most effective speakers against slavery, and was a Republican leader who believed in abolishing slavery through the machinery supplied by the Federal Constitution. In 1872 he was nominated for the Vice-Presidency on the ticket with Grant, and was elected. Not long afterward he was stricken with paralysis, and died in office. His nickname was an allusion to his early shoemaking days at Natick, Massachusetts.

SECTION I. The right of citizens of the United States to vote shall not be denied or abridged by the United States or by any State on account of race, color or previous condition of servitude.

Section II. The Congress shall have power to enforce this article by appropriate legislation.

Sir, it is now past six o'clock in the morning—a continuous session of more than eighteen hours. For more than seventeen hours the ear of the Senate has been wearied and pained with anti-republican, inhuman, and unchristian utterances, with the oft-repeated warnings, prophecies and predictions, with petty technicalities and carping criticisms. The majority in this Chamber, in the House, and in the country, too, have been arraigned, assailed and denounced, their ideas, principles and policies misrepresented, and their motives questioned. Sir, will our assailants never forget anything nor learn anything? Will they never see themselves as others see them? Year after year they have continuously and vehemently, as grand historic questions touching the interests of the country and the rights of our countrymen have arisen to be grappled with and solved, blurted into our unwilling ears these same warnings, prophecies and predictions, their unreasoning prejudices and passionate declamations. Time and events, which test all things, have brought discomfiture to their cause and made their illogical and ambitious rhetoric seem to be but weak and impotent drivel.

In spite of the discomfitures of the past, the champions of slavery and of the ideas, principles and policies pertaining to it are again doing battle for their perishing cause. Again, sir, we are arraigned, again misrepresented, again denounced. Why are we again thus misrepresented, arraigned and denounced? We, the friends of human rights, simply propose to submit to our countrymen an amendment of the Constitution of our country to secure the priceless boon of suffrage to citizens of the United States to whom the right to vote and be voted for is denied by the constitutions and laws of some of the States. This effort to remove the disabilities of the emancipated victims of the perished slave systems, to clothe them with power to maintain the dignity of manhood and

THE FIFTEENTH AMENDMENT 107

the honor and rights of citizenship, spring from our love of freedom, our sense of justice, our reverence for human nature, and our recognition of the fatherhood of God and the brotherhood of man. This effort, sanctified by patriotism, liberty, justice and humanity, is stigmatized in this Chamber as a mere partisan movement. Who make it a partisan movement? The men who are actuated by an imperative sense of duty, or the men who instinctively seize the occasion to arouse the unreasoning passions of race and caste and the prejudices of ignorance and hate? . . .

. . . Because frivolity and fashion put their ban upon the black man, be his character ever so pure or his intelligence ever so great, statesmen in this Christian land of republican institutions must deny to him civil and political rights and privileges. Because social life has put and continues to put its brand of exclusion upon the black man, it is therefore the duty of statesmanship to maintain by class legislation the abhorrent doctrine of caste in this Christian Republic. This is the argument, the logic, the position of Senators. . . .

Honorable Senators have grown weary in reminding us that it would be a breach of our plighted faith to submit to the State Legislatures this amendment to the Constitution to secure to American citizens the right to vote and to be voted for. They tell us we were pledged by our National Convention of 1868; that we were committed to the doctrine that the right to regulate the suffrage properly belonged to the loyal States. So the earlier Republican National Conventions proclaimed that slavery in the States was a local institution, for which the people of each State only were responsible. But that declaration did not stand in the way of the proclamation of emancipation, did not stand in the way of the thirteenth article of the amendments of the Constitution, did not stand in the way of that series of aggressive measures by which slavery was extirpated in the States. Slavery struck at the life of the nation, and the Republican party throttled its mortal foe. The Republican party in the National Convention of 1868 pronounced the guarantee by Congress of equal suffrage of all loyal men at the South as demanded by every consideration of public safety, gratitude, and of justice, and determined that it should be maintained. That declaration unreservedly committed the Republican party to the safety and justice of equal suffrage. The declaration that the suffrage in the loyal States properly belonged to the people of those States meant this, no more, no less: that under the Constitution it belonged to the people of each of the loyal States to regulate suffrage therein. . . .

Senators accuse us of being actuated by partisanship, by the love of power, and the hope of retaining power; yet they never tire of reminding us that the people have in several States pronounced against equal suffrage and will do so again. I took occasion early in the debate to express the opinion that in the series of measures for the extirpation of slavery and the elevation and enfranchisement of the black race the Republican party had lost at least a quarter of a million of voters. In every great battle of the last eight years the timid, the weak faltered, fell back or slunk away into the ranks of the enemy. Yes, sir; while we have been struggling often against fearful odds, timid men, weak men and bad men, too, following the examples of timid men, weak men and bad men in all the great struggles for the rights of human nature, have broken from our advancing ranks and fallen back to the rear or gone over to the enemy, thus giving to the foe the strength they had pledged to us. But we have gone on prospering, and we shall go on prospering in spite of treacheries on the right hand and on the left. The timid may chide us, the weak reproach us, and the bad malign us, but we shall strive on, for in struggling to secure and protect the rights of others we assure our own.

THE KU-KLUX KLAN

By the Federal Grand Jury

SOUTHERN opposition to the fourteenth amendment to the Constitution took the form of secret societies, whose members were sworn to curb the negroes in the use, or rather abuse, of their newly acquired citizenship, and also to put down both the "carpet-baggers" and their Southern supporters, the "scalawags." Chief among these societies was the Ku-Klux Klan, which originated in Tennessee but quickly extended its "invisible empire" over the South. Its activities in South Carolina, where the worst results of carpet-bag government were seen, caused President Grant, under the authority given him by the Ku-Klux Act of 1871 to enforce the fourteenth amendment, to suspend the habeas corpus privilege. Federal judges were authorized to exclude from juries those who were believed to be accomplices of persons engaged in committing Ku-Klux outrages.

The accompanying presentment was made in the Circuit Court at Columbia, South Carolina, after the privilege of the habeas corpus writ had been suspended.

TO the Judges of the United States Circuit Court: In closing the labors of the present term, the grand jury beg leave to submit the following presentment: During the whole session we have been engaged in investigations of the most grave and extraordinary character—investigations of the crimes committed by the organization known as the Ku-Klux Klan. The evidence elicited has been voluminous, gathered from the victims themselves and their families, as well as those who belong to the Klan and participated in its crimes. The jury has been shocked beyond measure at the developments which have been made in their presence of the number and character of the atrocities committed, producing a state of terror and a sense of utter insecurity among a large portion of the people, especially the colored population. The evidence produced before us has established the following facts:

1. That there has existed since 1868, in many counties of the State, an organization known as the "Ku-Klux Klan," or "Invisible Empire of the South," which embraces in its membership a large proportion of the white population of every profession and class.

2. That this Klan [is] bound together by an oath, administered to its members at the time of their initiation into the order, of which the following is a copy:

Obligation

I, (name,) before the immaculate Judge of Heaven and Earth, and upon the Holy Evangelists of Almighty God, do, of my own free will and accord, subscribe to the following sacredly binding obligation:

"1. We are on the side of justice, humanity, and constitutional liberty, as bequeathed to us in its purity by our forefathers.

"2. We oppose and reject the principles of the radical party.

"3. We pledge mutual aid to each other in sickness, distress, and pecuniary embarrassment.

"4. Female friends, widows, and their households, shall ever be special objects of our regard and protection.

"Any member divulging, or causing to be divulged, any of the foregoing obligations, shall meet the fearful penalty and traitor's doom, which is Death! Death! Death!"

That in addition to this oath the Klan has a constitution and by-laws, which provides, among other things, that each member shall furnish himself with a pistol, a Ku-Klux gown, and a signal instrument. That the operations of the Klan were executed in the night, and were invariably directed against members of the republican party by warnings to leave the country, by whippings, and by murder.

3. That in large portions of the counties of York, Union and Spartanburgh, to which our attention has been more particularly called in our investigations during part of the time for the last eighteen months, the civil law has been set at defiance, and ceased to afford any protection to the citizens.

4. That the Klan, in carrying out the purposes for which it was organized and armed, inflicted summary vengeance on the colored citizens of these counties, by breaking into their houses at the dead of night, dragging them from their beds, torturing them in the most inhuman manner, and in many instances murdering them; and this, mainly, on account of their political affiliations. Occasionally additional reasons operated, but in no instance was the political feature wanting.

5. That for this condition of things, for all these violations of law and order, and the sacred rights of

citizens, many of the leading men of those counties were responsible. It was proven that large numbers of the most prominent citizens were members of the order. Many of this class attended meetings of the Grand Klan. At a meeting of the Grand Klan, held in Spartanburgh County, at which there were representatives from the various dens of Spartanburgh, York, Union and Chester Counties, in this State, besides a number from North Carolina, a resolution was adopted that no raids should be undertaken, or any one whipped or injured by members of the Klan, without orders from the Grand Klan. The penalty for violating this resolution was one hundred lashes on the bare back for the first offense, and for the second, death. This testimony establishes the nature of the discipline enforced in the order, and also the fact that many of the men who were openly and publicly speaking against the Klan, and pretending to deplore the work of this murderous conspiracy, were influential members of the order, and directing its operations even in detail.

The jury has been appalled as much at the number of outrages as at their character, it appearing that eleven murders and over six hundred whippings have been committed in York County alone. Our investigation in regard to the other counties named has been less full; but it is believed, from the testimony, that an equal or greater number has been committed in Union, and that the number is not greatly less in Spartanburgh and Laurens.

We are of the opinion that the most vigorous prosecution of the parties implicated in these crimes is imperatively demanded; that without this there is greater danger that these outrages will be continued, and that there will be no security to our fellow-citizens of African descent.

We would say further, that unless the strong arm of the Government is interposed to punish these crimes committed upon this class of citizens, there is every reason to believe that an organized and determined attempt at retaliation will be made, which can only result in a state of anarchy and bloodshed too horrible to contemplate.

THE GENEVA AWARD IN THE "ALABAMA" CLAIMS

By the Arbitrators

BY the terms of the Treaty of Washington the claims of the United States against Great Britain, arising out of depredations committed during the Civil War on American commerce by the Alabama and other cruisers fitted out in England, were submitted to arbitration. There were five arbitrators, four of whom, headed by Charles Francis Adams, the American representative, signed the accompanying document of award, September 14, 1872, at Geneva. The other signers were Count Frederick Sclopis, of Italy; Jacob Stämpfli, of Switzerland, and Vicomte d'Itajuba, of Brazil. The British arbitrator, Sir Alexander Cockburn, refused to sign it.

Of the several English-built-and-manned cruisers involved in the controversy, the Alabama alone is said to have captured and destroyed seventy American vessels. The court awarded $15,500,000 as a full indemnity of all claims against Britain.

THE United States of America and Her Britannic Majesty having agreed by Article I of the treaty concluded and signed at Washington the 8th of May, 1871, to refer all the claims "generally known as the Alabama claims" to a tribunal of arbitration. . . .

And the five arbitrators . . . having assembled at Geneva . . . on the 15th of December, 1871. . . .

The agents named by each of the high contracting parties . . . then delivered to each of the arbitrators the printed case prepared by each of the two parties, accompanied by the documents, the official correspondence, and other evidence on which each relied, in conformity with the terms of the third article of the said treaty. . . .

The tribunal, in accordance with the vote of adjournment passed at their second session, held on the 16th of December, 1871, reassembled at Geneva on the 15th of June, 1872; and the agent of each of the parties duly delivered to each of the arbitrators, and to the agent of the other party, the printed argument referred to in Article V of the said treaty.

The tribunal having since fully taken into their consideration the treaty, and also the cases, counter-cases, documents, evidence and arguments, and likewise all other communications made to them by the two parties during the progress of their sittings, and having impartially and carefully examined the same,

Has arrived at the decision embodied in the present award:

Whereas, having regard to the VIth and VIIth articles of the said treaty, the arbitrators are bound under the terms of the said VIth article, "in deciding the matters submitted to them, to be governed by the three rules therein specified and by such principles of international law, not inconsistent therewith, as the arbitrators shall determine to have been applicable to the case";

["Rules.—A neutral Government is bound—

"First, to use due diligence to prevent the fitting out, arming, or equipping, within its jurisdiction, of any vessel which it has reasonable ground to believe is intended to cruise or to carry on war against a Power with which it is at peace; and also to use like diligence to prevent the departure from its jurisdiction of any vessel intended to cruise or carry on war as above, such vessel having been specially adapted, in whole or in part, within such jurisdiction, to warlike use.

"Secondly, not to permit or suffer either belligerent to make use of its ports or waters as the base of naval operations against the other, or for the purpose of the renewal or augmentation of military supplies or arms, or the recruitment of men.

"Thirdly, to exercise due diligence in its own ports and waters, and, as to all persons within its jurisdiction, to prevent any violation of the foregoing obligations and duties."]

And whereas the "due diligence" referred to in the first and third of the said rules ought to be exercised by neutral governments in exact proportion to the risks to which either of the belligerents may be exposed, from a failure to fulfil the obligations of neutrality on their part;

And whereas the circumstances out of which the facts constituting the subject-matter of the present controversy arose were of a nature to call for the exercise on the part of Her Britannic Majesty's government of all possible solicitude for the observance of the rights and the duties involved in the proclamation of neutrality issued by Her Majesty on the 13th day of May, 1861;

And whereas the effects of a violation of neutrality committed by means of the construction, equipment, and armament of a vessel are not done away with by any commission which the government of the belligerent power, benefited by the violation of neutrality, may afterwards have granted to that vessel; and the ultimate step, by which the offense is completed, cannot be admissible as a ground for the absolution of the offender, nor can the consummation of his fraud become the means of establishing his innocence;

And whereas the privilege of exterritoriality accorded to vessels of war has been admitted into the law of nations, not as an absolute right, but solely as a proceeding founded on the principle of courtesy and mutual deference between different nations, and therefore can never be appealed to for the protection of acts done in violation of neutrality;

And whereas the absence of a previous notice cannot be regarded as a failure in any consideration required by the law of nations, in those cases in which a vessel carries with it its own condemnation;

And whereas, in order to impart to any supplies of coal a character inconsistent with the second rule, prohibiting the use of neutral ports or waters, as a base of naval operations for a belligerent, it is necessary that the said supplies should be connected with special circumstances of time, of persons, or of place, which may combine to give them such character;

And whereas, with respect to the vessel called the "Alabama," it clearly results from all the facts relative to the construction of the ship at first designated by the number "290" in the port of Liverpool, and its equipment and armament in the vicinity of Terceira through the agency of the vessels called the "Agrippina" and the "Bahama," dispatched from Great Britain to that end, that the British government failed to use due diligence in the performance of its neutral obligations; and especially that it omitted, notwithstanding the warnings and official representations made by the diplomatic agents of the United States during the construction of the said number "290," to take in due time any effective measures of prevention, and that those orders which it did give at last, for the detention of the vessel, were issued so late that their execution was not practicable;

And whereas, after the escape of that vessel, the measures taken for its pursuit and arrest were so imperfect as to lead to no result, and therefore cannot be considered sufficient to release Great Britain from the responsibility already incurred;

And whereas, in despite of the violations of the neutrality of Great Britain committed by the "290," this same vessel, later known as the Confederate cruiser "Alabama," was on several occasions freely admitted into the ports of colonies of Great Britain, instead of being proceeded against as it ought to have been in any and every port within British jurisdiction in which it might have been found;

And whereas the government of Her Britannic Majesty cannot justify itself for a failure in due diligence on the plea of insufficiency of the legal means of action which it possessed:

Four of the arbitrators, for the reasons above assigned, and the fifth for reasons separately assigned by him,

Are of opinion—

That Great Britain has in this case failed, by omission, to fulfill the duties prescribed in the first and the third of the rules established by the VIth article of the Treaty of Washington.

And whereas, with respect to the vessel called the "Florida," it results from all the facts relative to the construction of the "Oreto" in the port of Liverpool, and to its issue therefrom, which facts failed to induce the authorities in Great Britain to resort to measures adequate to prevent the violation of the neutrality of that nation, notwithstanding the warnings and repeated representations of the agents of the United States, that Her Majesty's government has failed to use due diligence to fulfil the duties of neutrality;

And whereas it likewise results from all the facts relative to the stay of the "Oreto" at Nassau, to her issue from that port, to her enlistment of men, to her supplies, and to her armament, with the coöperation of the British vessel "Prince Alfred," at Green Cay, that there was negligence on the part of the British colonial authorities;

And whereas, notwithstanding the violation of the neutrality of Great Britain committed by the "Oreto," this same vessel, later known as the Confederate cruiser "Florida," was nevertheless on several occasions freely admitted into the ports of British colonies;

And whereas the judicial acquittal of the "Oreto" at Nassau cannot relieve Great Britain from the responsibility incurred by her under the principles of international law; nor can the fact of the entry of the "Florida" into the Confederate port of Mobile, and of its stay there during four months, extinguish the responsibility previously to that time incurred by Great Britain:

For these reasons,

The tribunal, by a majority of four voices to one, is of opinion—

That Great Britain has in this case failed, by omission, to fulfil the duties prescribed in the first, in the second, and in the third of the rules established by Article VI of the Treaty of Washington.

And whereas, with respect to the vessel called the "Shenandoah," it results from all the facts relative to the departure from London of the merchant-vessel the "Sea King," and to the transformation of that ship into a confederate cruiser under the name of the "Shenandoah," near the island of Madeira, that the government of Her Britannic Majesty is not chargeable with any failure, down to that date, in the use of due diligence to fulfil the duties of neutrality;

But whereas it results from all the facts connected with the stay of the "Shenandoah" at Melbourne, and especially with the augmentation which the British government itself admits to have been clandestinely effected of her force, by the enlistment of men within that port, that there was negligence on the part of the authorities at that place:

For these reasons,

The tribunal is unanimously of opinion—

That Great Britain has not failed, by any act or omission, "to fulfil any of the duties prescribed by the three rules of Article VI in the Treaty of Washington, or by the principles of international law not inconsistent therewith," in respect to the vessel called the "Shenandoah," during the period of time anterior to her entry into the port of Melbourne;

And, by a majority of three to two voices, the tribunal decides that Great Britain has failed, by omission, to fulfill the duties prescribed by the second and third of the rules aforesaid, in the case of this same vessel, from and after her entry into Hobson's Bay, and is therefore responsible for all acts committed by that vessel after her departure from Melbourne, on the 18th day of February, 1865.

And so far as relates to the vessels called—

The "Tuscaloosa," (tender to the "Alabama,")

The "Clarence,"

The "Tacony," and

The "Archer," (tenders to the "Florida,")

The tribunal is unanimously of opinion—

That such tenders or auxiliary vessels, being properly regarded as accessories, must necessarily follow the lot of their principals, and be submitted to the same decision which applies to them respectively.

And so far as relates to the vessel called "Retribution,"

The tribunal, by a majority of three to two voices, is of opinion—

That Great Britain has not failed by any act or omission to fulfil any of the duties prescribed by the three rules of Article VI in the treaty of Washington, or by the principles of international law not inconsistent therewith.

And so far as relates to the vessels called—
The "Georgia,"
The "Sumter,"
The "Nashville,"
The "Tallahassee," and
The "Chickamauga," respectively,
The tribunal is unanimously of opinion—

That Great Britain has not failed, by any act or omission, to fulfil any of the duties prescribed by the three rules of Article VI in the Treaty of Washington, or by the principles of international law not inconsistent therewith.

And so far as relates to the vessels called—
The "Sallie,"
The "Jefferson Davis,"
The "Music,"
The "Boston," and
The "V. H. Joy," respectively,
The tribunal is unanimously of opinion—

That they ought to be excluded from consideration for want of evidence.

And whereas, so far as relates to the particulars of the indemnity claimed by the United States, the costs of pursuit of the Confederate cruisers are not, in the judgment of the tribunal, properly distinguishable from the general expenses of the war carried on by the United States:

The tribunal is, therefore, of opinion, by a majority of three to two voices—

That there is no ground for awarding to the United States any sum by way of indemnity under this head.

And whereas prospective earnings cannot properly be made the subject of compensation, inasmuch as they depend in their nature upon future and uncertain contingencies:

The tribunal is unanimously of opinion—

That there is no ground for awarding to the United States any sum by way of indemnity under this head.

And whereas, in order to arrive at an equitable compensation for the damages which have been sustained, it is necessary to set aside all double claims for the same losses, and all claims for "gross freights," so far as they exceed "net freights";

And whereas it is just and reasonable to allow interest at a reasonable rate;

And whereas, in accordance with the spirit and letter of the Treaty of Washington, it is preferable to adopt the form of adjudication of a sum in gross, rather than to refer the subject of compensation for further discussion and deliberation to a board of assessors, as provided by Article X of the said treaty:

The tribunal, making use of the authority conferred upon it by Article VII of the said treaty, by a majority of four voices to one, awards to the United States a sum of $15,500,000 in gold, as the indemnity to be paid by Great Britain to the United States, for the satisfaction of all the claims referred to the consideration of the tribunal, conformably to the provisions contained in Article VII of the aforesaid treaty.

And, in accordance with the terms of Article XI of the said treaty, the tribunal declares that "all the claims referred to in the treaty as submitted to the tribunal are hereby fully, perfectly, and finally settled."

Furthermore it declares, that "each and every one of the said claims, whether the same may or may not have been presented to the notice of, or made, preferred, or laid before the tribunal, shall henceforth be considered and treated as finally settled, barred, and inadmissible." . . .

Made and concluded at the Hôtel de Ville of Geneva, in Switzerland, the 14th day of the month of September, in the year of our Lord one thousand eight hundred and seventy-two.

      CHARLES FRANCIS ADAMS.
      FREDERICK SCLOPIS.
      STÄMPFLI.
      VICOMTE D'ITAJUBÁ.

THE GREAT CHICAGO FIRE

By Horace White

WHITE *was editor-in-chief of the* Chicago Tribune, *in the office of which, October 14, 1871, he wrote this eye-witness account of the most destructive conflagration in American history. It was written as a letter to Murat Halstead, then editor of the* Cincinnati Commercial. *White had accompanied Abraham Lincoln, in 1858, in his campaign against Stephen A. Douglas, and his account of that celebrated contest appears in Herndon's "Life of Lincoln." Moving to New York six years after the great Chicago fire, White joined with Carl Schurz and Edwin L. Godkin in producing the New York* Evening Post, *of which he eventually succeeded Godkin as editor-in-chief.*

Starting in a barn in De Koven Street, the Chicago fire raged for two days and nights, sweeping over 2,100 acres, destroying 17,450 buildings, and causing 200 deaths, besides the greatest destitution and suffering. More than 70,000 were rendered homeless, out of a population of 324,000.

AS a slight acknowledgment of your thoughtful kindness in forwarding to us, without orders, a complete outfit of type and cases, when you heard that we had been burned out, I send you a hastily written sketch of what I saw at the great fire. . . .

The history of the great fire in Chicago, which rises to the dignity of a national event, cannot be written until each witness, who makes any record whatever, shall have told what he saw. Nobody could see it all—no more than one man could see the whole of the Battle of Gettysburg. It was too vast, too swift, too full of smoke, too full of danger, for anybody to see it all. My experience derives its only public importance from the fact that what I did, substantially, a hundred thousand others did or attempted—that is, saved or sought to save their lives and enough of their wearing-apparel to face the sky in. . . .

I had retired to rest, though not to sleep (Sunday, October 8) when the great bell struck the alarm, but fires had been so frequent of late, and had been so speedily extinguished, that I did not deem it worth while to get up and look at it, or even to count the strokes on the bell to learn where it was. The bell paused for fifteen minutes before giving the general alarm, which distinguishes a great fire from a small one. When it sounded the general alarm I rose and looked out. There was a great light to the southwest of my residence, but no greater than I had frequently seen in that quarter, where vast piles of pine lumber have been stored all the time I have lived in Chicago, some eighteen years. But it was not pine lumber that was burning this time. It was a row of wooden tenements in the South Division of the city, in which a few days ago were standing whole rows of the most costly buildings which it has entered into the hearts of architects to conceive. I watched the increasing light for a few moments. Red tongues of light began to shoot upward; my family were all aroused by this time, and I dressed myself for the purpose of going to the "Tribune" office to write something about the catastrophe. Once out upon the street, the magnitude of the fire was suddenly disclosed to me.

The dogs of hell were upon the housetops of La Salle and Wells streets, just south of Adams, bounding from one to another. The fire was moving northward like ocean surf on a sand beach. It had already traveled an eighth of a mile and was far beyond control. A column of flame would shoot up from a burning building, catch the force of the wind, and strike the next one, which in turn would perform the same direful office for its neighbor. It was simply indescribable in its terrible grandeur. Vice and crime had got the first scorching. The district where the fire got its first firm foothold was the Alsatia of Chicago. Fleeing before it was a crowd of blear-eyed, drunken and diseased wretches, male and female, half-naked, ghastly, with painted cheeks, cursing and uttering ribald jests as they drifted along.

I went to the "Tribune" office, ascended to the editorial rooms, took the only inflammable thing there, a kerosene lamp, and carried it to the basement, where I emptied the oil into the sewer. This was scarcely done when I perceived the flames breaking out of the roof of the court house, the old nucleus of which, in the center of the edifice, was not constructed of fireproof material, as the new wings had been. As the flames had leapt a vacant space of nearly two hundred feet to get at this roof, it was evident that most of the business portion of the city must go down, but I did not reflect that the city water works, with their four great pumping engines, were in a straight line with the fire and wind. Nor did I know then that this

THE CHICAGO FIRE
From a contemporary engraving

priceless machinery was covered by a wooden roof. The flames were driving thither with demon precision.

Billows of fire were rolling over the business palaces of the city and swallowing up their contents. Walls were falling so fast that the quaking of the ground under our feet was scarcely noticed, so continuous was the reverberation. Sober men and women were hurrying through the streets from the burning quarter, some with bundles of clothes on their shoulders, others dragging trunks along the sidewalks by means of strings and ropes fastened to the handles, children trudging by their sides or borne in their arms. Now and then a sick man or woman would be observed, half concealed in a mattress doubled up and borne by two men. Droves of horses were in the streets, moving by some sort of guidance to a place of safety. Vehicles of all descriptions were hurrying to and fro, some laden with trunks and bundles, others seeking similar loads and immediately finding them, the drivers making more money in one hour than they were used to see in a week or a month. Everybody in this quarter was hurrying toward the lake shore. All the streets crossing that part of Michigan Avenue, which fronts on the lake (on which my own residence stood) were crowded with fugitives, hastening toward the blessed water.

We saw the tall buildings on the opposite sides of the two streets melt down in a few moments without scorching ours. The heat broke the plate-glass windows in the lower stories, but not in the upper ones.

After the fire in our neighborhood had spent its force, the editorial and composing rooms did not even smell of smoke. Several of our brave fellows who had been up all night had gone to sleep on the lounges, while others were at the sink washing their faces, supposing that all danger to us had passed. So I supposed, and in this belief went home to breakfast. The smoke to the northward was so dense that we could not see the North Division, where sixty thousand people were flying in mortal terror before the flames. The immense store of Field, Leiter & Co. I observed to be under a shower of water from their own fire-apparatus, and since the First National Bank, a fire-proof building, protected it on one corner, I concluded that the progress of the flames in that direction was stopped, as the "Tribune" building had stopped it where we were. Here, at least, I thought was a saving of twenty millions of property, including the great Central depot and the two grain-elevators adjoining, effected by two or three buildings which had been erected with a view to such an emergency. The post-office and custom-house building (also fire-proof, according to public rumor) had stopped the flames a little farther to the southwest, although the interior of that structure was burning. A straight line drawn northeast from the post-office would nearly touch the "Tribune," First National Bank, Field, Leiter & Co.'s store, and the Illinois Central Railroad land department, another fire-proof. Everything east of that line seemed perfectly safe. And with this feeling I went home to breakfast.

There was still a mass of fire to the southwest, in the direction whence it originally came, but as the engines were all down there, and the buildings small and low, I felt sure that the firemen would manage it. As soon as I had swallowed a cup of coffee and communicated to my family the facts that I had gathered, I started out to see the end of the battle. Reaching State Street, I glanced down to Field, Leiter & Co.'s store, and to my surprise noticed that the streams of water which had before been showering it, as though it had been a great artificial fountain, had ceased to run. But I did not conjecture the awful reality, viz., that the great pumping engines had been disabled by a burning roof falling upon them. I thought perhaps the firemen on the store had discontinued their efforts because the danger was over. But why were men carrying out goods from the lower story?

This query was soon answered by a gentleman who asked me if I had heard that the water had stopped! The awful truth was here! The pumping engines were disabled, and though we had at our feet a basin sixty miles wide by three hundred and sixty long, and seven hundred feet deep, all full of clear green water, we could not lift enough to quench a cooking-stove. Still the direction of the wind was such that I thought the remaining fire would not cross State Street, nor reach the residences on Wabash and

Michigan avenues and the terrified people on the lake shore. I determined to go down to the black cloud of smoke which was rising away to the southwest, the course of which could not be discovered on account of the height of the intervening buildings, but thought it most prudent to go home again, and tell my wife to get the family wearing-apparel in readiness for moving. I found that she had already done so. I then hurried toward the black cloud, some ten squares distant, and there found the rows of wooden houses on Third and Fourth avenues falling like ripe wheat before the reaper. At a glance I perceived that all was lost in our part of the city, and I conjectured that the "Tribune" building was doomed too, for I had noticed with consternation that the fire-proof postoffice had been completely gutted, notwithstanding it was detached from other buildings. The "Tribune" was fitted into a niche, one side of which consisted of a wholesale stationery store, and the other of McVicker's Theater. But there was now no time to think of property. Life was in danger. The lives of those most dear to me depended upon their getting out of our house, out of our street, through an infernal gorge of horses, wagons, men, women, children, trunks and plunder.

My brother was with me, and we seized the first empty wagon we could find, pinning the horse by the head. A hasty talk with the driver disclosed that we could have his establishment for one load for twenty dollars. I had not expected to get him for less than a hundred, unless we should take him by force, and this was a bad time for a fight. He proved himself a muscular as well as a faithful fellow, and I shall always be glad that I avoided a personal difficulty with him. One peculiarity of the situation was that nobody could get a team without ready money. I had not thought of this when I was revolving in my mind the offer of one hundred dollars, which was more greenbacks than our whole family could have put up if our lives had depended upon the issue. This driver had divined that, as all the banks were burned, a check on the Commercial National would not carry him very far, although it might carry me to a place of safety. All the drivers had divined the same. Every man who had anything to sell perceived the same. "Pay as you go" had become the watchword of the hour. Never was there a community so hastily and so completely emancipated from the evils of the credit system.

With some little difficulty we reached our house, and in less time than we ever set out on a journey before, we dragged seven trunks, four bundles, four valises, two baskets, and one hamper of provisions into the street and piled them on the wagon. The fire was still more than a quarter of a mile distant, and the wind, which was increasing in violence, was driving it not exactly in our direction. The low wooden houses were nearly all gone, and after that the fire must make progress, if at all, against brick and stone. Several churches of massive architecture were between us and harm, and the great Palmer House had not been reached, and might not be if the firemen, who had now got their hose into the lake, could work efficiently in the ever-increasing jam of fugitives.

My wife thought we should have time to take another load; my brother thought so; we all thought so. We had not given due credit either to the savage strength of the fire or the firm pack on Michigan Avenue. Leaving my brother to get the family safely out if I did not return in time, and to pile the most valuable portion of my library into the drawers of bureaus and tables ready for moving, I seized a bird-cage containing a talented green parrot, and mounted the seat with the driver. For one square southward from the corner of Monroe Street we made pretty fair progress. The dust was so thick that we could not see the distance of a whole square ahead. It came, not in clouds, but in a steady storm of sand, the particles impinging against our faces like needle-points. Pretty soon we came to a dead halt. We could move neither forward, nor backward, nor sidewise. The gorge had caught fast somewhere. Yet everybody was good-natured and polite. If I should say I didn't hear an oath all the way down Michigan Avenue, there are probably some mule-drivers in Cincinnati who would say it was a lie. But I did not. The only quarrelsome person I saw was a German laborer (a noted exception to his race), who was protesting that he had lost everything, and that he would not get out of the middle of the road although he was on foot. He became obstreperous on this point, and commenced beating the head of my horse with his fist. My driver was preparing to knock him down with the butt-end of the whip, when two men seized the insolent Teuton and dragged him to the water's edge, where it is to be hoped he was ducked.

Presently the jam began to move, and we got on perhaps twenty paces and stuck fast again. By accident we had edged over to the east side of the street, and nothing but a board fence separated us from the lake park, a strip of ground a little wider than the street itself. A benevolent laborer on the park side of the fence pulled a loose post from the ground, and with this for a catapult knocked off the boards and invited us to pass through. It was a hazardous undertaking, as we had to drive diagonally over a raised sidewalk, but we thought it was best to risk it. Our horse mounted and gave us a jerk which nearly threw us off the seat, and sent the provision basket and one bundle of clothing whirling into the dirt. The eatables were irrecoverable. The bundle was rescued, with two or three pounds of butter plastered upon it. We started again, and here our parrot broke out with great rapidity and sharpness of utterance, "Get up, get up, get up, hurry up, hurry up, it's eight o'clock," ending with a shrill whistle. These ejaculations frightened a pair of carriage-horses, close to us, on the other side of the fence, but the jam was so tight they couldn't run.

By getting into the park we succeeded in advancing two squares without impediment, and we might have gone farther had we not come upon an excavation which the public authorities had recently made. This drove us back to the avenue, where another battering-ram made a gap for us at the intersection of Van Buren Street, the north end of Michigan Terrace. Here the gorge seemed impassable. The difficulty proceeded from teams entering Michigan Avenue from cross-streets. Extempore policemen stationed themselves at these crossings and helped, as well as they could, but we were half an hour passing the terrace. From this imposing row of residences the millionaires were dragging their trunks and their bundles, and yet there was no panic, no frenzy, no boisterousness, but only the haste which the situation authorized. There was real danger to life all along this street, but nobody realized it, because the park was ample to hold all the people. None of us asked or thought what would become of those nearest the water if the smoke and cinders should drive the whole crowd down to the shore, or if the vast bazaar of luggage should itself take fire, as some of it afterward did. Fortunately for those in the street, there was a limit to the number of teams available in that quarter of the city. The contributions from the cross-streets grew less; and soon we began to move on a walk without interruption.

At Eldridge Court, I turned into Wabash Avenue, where the crowd was thinner. Arriving at the house of a friend, who was on the windward side of the fire, I tumbled off my load and started back to get another. Half-way down Michigan Avenue, which was now perceptibly easier to move in, I perceived my family on the sidewalk with their arms full of light household effects. My wife told me that the house was already burned, that the flames burst out ready-made in the rear hall before she knew that the roof had been scorched, and that one of the servants, who had disobeyed orders in her eagerness to save some article, had got singed, though not burned, in coming out. My wife and my mother and all the rest were begrimed with dirt and smoke, like blackamoors; everybody was. The "bloated aristocrats" all along the streets, who supposed they had lost both home and fortune at one swoop, were a sorry but not despairing congregation. They had saved their lives at all events, and they knew that many of their fellow creatures must have lost theirs. I saw a great many kindly acts done as we moved along. The poor helped the rich, and the rich helped the poor (if anybody could be called rich at such a time), to get on with their loads. I heard of cartmen demanding one hundred and fifty dollars (in hand, of course) for carrying a single load. Very likely it was so, but those cases did not come under my own notice. It did come under my notice that some cartmen worked for whatever the sufferers felt able to pay, and one I knew worked with alacrity for nothing. It takes all sorts of people to make a great fire.

Presently we heard loud detonations, and a rumor went around that buildings were being blown up with gunpowder. The depot of the Hazard Powder Company was situated at Brighton, seven or eight miles from the nearest point of the fire. At what time the effort was first made to reach this magazine, and bring powder into the service, I have not learned, but I know that Col. M. C. Stearns made heroic efforts with his great lime-wagons to haul the explosive material to the proper point.

This is no time to blame anybody, but in truth there was no directing head on the ground. Everybody was asking everybody else to pull down buildings. There were no hooks, no ropes, no axes. I had met General Sheridan on the street in front of the post-office two hours before. He had been trying to save the army records, including his own invaluable papers relating to the war of the rebellion. He told me they were all lost, and then added that "the post-office didn't seem to make a good fire." This was when we supposed the row of fire-proof buildings, already spoken of, had stopped the flames in our quarter. Where was General Sheridan now? everybody asked. Why didn't he do something when everybody else had failed? Presently a rumor went around that Sheridan was handling the gunpowder; then everybody felt relieved. The reverberations of the powder, whoever was handling it, gave us all heart again. Think of a people feeling encouraged because somebody was blowing up houses in the midst of the city,

THE GREAT CHICAGO FIRE 139

and that a shower of bricks was very likely to come down on their heads!

I had paid and discharged my driver after extorting his solemn promise to come back and move me again if the wind should shift to the north—in which event everybody knew that the whole South Division, for a distance of four miles, must perish. We soon arrived at the house of the kind friend on Wabash Avenue, where our trunks and bundles had been deposited. This was south of the line of fire, but this did not satisfy anybody, since we had all seen how resolutely the flames had gone transversely across the direction of the wind. Then came a story from down the street that Sheridan was going to blow up the Wabash Avenue Methodist Church on the corner of Harrison Street. We observed a general scattering away of people from that neighborhood. I was nearly four squares south of the locality, and thought that the missiles wouldn't come so far. We awaited the explosion, but it did not come. By and by we plucked up courage to go around two or three blocks and see whether the church had fallen down of its own accord.

We perceived that two or three houses in the rear of the edifice had been leveled to the ground, that the church itself was standing, and that the fire was out, in that quarter at least; also, that the line of Harrison Street marked the southern limits of the devastation. The wind continued to blow fiercely from the southwest, and has not ceased to this hour (Saturday, October 14). But it was liable to change. If it chopped around to the north, the burning embers would be blown back upon the South Division. If it veered to the east, they would be blown into the West Division, though the river afforded rather better protection there. Then we should have nothing to do but to keep ahead of the flames and get down as fast as possible to the open prairie, and there spend the night houseless and supperless—and what of the morrow? A full hundred thousand of us. And if we were spared, and the West Division were driven out upon their prairie (a hundred and fifty thousand according to the Federal census), how would the multitude be fed? If there could be anything more awful than what we had already gone through, it would be what we would certainly go through if the wind should change; for with the embers of this great fire flying about, and no water to fight them, we knew that there was not gunpowder enough in Illinois to stop the inevitable conflagration. But this was not all.

A well-authenticated rumor came up to the city that the prairie was on fire south of Hyde Park, the largest of the southern suburbs. The grass was as dry as tinder, and so were the leaves in Cottage Grove, a piece of timber several miles square, containing hundreds of residences of the better class, some of them of palatial dimensions. A fire on the prairie, communicating itself to the grove, might cut off the retreat of the one hundred thousand people in the South Division; might invade the South Division itself, and come up under the impulse of that fierce wind, and where should we all be then? There were three or four bridges leading to the West Division, the only possible avenues of escape; but what were these among so many? And what if the "Commune" should go to work and start incendiary fires while all was yet in confusion? These fiends were improving the daylight by plundering along the street. Before dark the whole male population of the city was organized by spontaneous impulse into a night patrol, with pallid determination to put every incendiary to instant death.

About five o'clock P. M. I applied to a friend on Wabash Avenue for the use of a team to convey my family and chattels to the southern suburbs, about four miles distant, where my brother happened to own a small cottage, which, up to the present time, nobody could be induced to occupy and pay rent for. My friend replied that his work-teams were engaged hauling water for people to drink. Here was another thing that I had not thought of—a great city with no water to drink. Plenty in the lake, to be sure, but none in the city mains or the connecting pipes. Fortunately the extreme western limits were provided with a number of artesian wells, bored for manufacturing establishments. Then there was the river—the horrible, black, stinking river of a few weeks ago, which has since become clear enough for fish to live in, by reason of the deepening of the canal, which draws to the Mississippi a perpetual flow of pure water from Lake Michigan. With the city pumping-works stopped, the sewers could no longer discharge themselves into the river. So this might be used; and it was. Twenty-four hours had not passed before tens of thousands of people were drinking the water of Chicago River, with no unpleasant taste or effects.

The work-teams of my friend being engaged in hauling water for people who could not get any from the wells or the river or lake, he placed at my disposal his carriage, horses and coachman, whom he directed to take me and the ladies to any place we desired to reach. While we were talking he hailed another gentleman on the street, who owned a large stevedore wagon, and asked him to convey my trunks, etc., to Cottage Grove Avenue, near Forty-third Street, to which request an immediate and most gracious assent was given. And thus we started again, our hostess pressing a mattress upon us from her store. All the streets leading southward were yet filled with fugitives. Where they all found shelter that night I know not, but every house seemed to be opened to anybody who desired to enter. Arrived at our new home, about dusk, we found in it, as we expected, a cold reception, there being neither stove, nor grate, nor fireplace, nor fuel, nor light therein. But I will not dwell upon these things. We really did not mind them, for when we thought of the thousands of men, women, and tender babes huddled together in Lincoln Park, seven miles to the north of us, with no prospect of food, exposed to rain, if it should come, with no canopy but the driving smoke of their homes, we thought how little we had suffered.

THE GREELEY CAMPAIGN
By James G. Blaine

BLAINE, from whose "Twenty Years of Congress" this account is taken by permission of the copyright-holders, was a member of Congress during the Grant-Greeley campaign of 1872. As Speaker of the House during three of his seven successive terms in Congress, he became a power and his conduct was uniformly marked by great readiness and ability.

Blaine, although a political opponent of Greeley in this campaign, does not conceal his admiration for the sterling character and journalistic ability of the famous editor of the New York Tribune. To Greeley the campaign was disastrous in more ways than one. Not only was he overwhelmingly defeated, but the contest overtaxed his strength and left him a mental and physical wreck. Near its close he lost his wife, and he himself died within a month after President Grant was re-elected.

WITH Grant and Greeley fairly in the field, the country entered upon a remarkable contest. At the beginning of the picturesque and emotional "log cabin canvass of 1840," Mr. Van Buren, with his keen insight into popular movements, had said, in somewhat mixed metaphor, that it would be "either a farce or a tornado." The present canvass gave promise on different grounds of similar alternatives. General Grant had been tried, and with him the country knew what to expect. Mr. Greeley had not been tried, and though the best known man in his own field of journalism, he was the least known and most doubted in the field of governmental administration. No other candidate could have presented such an antithesis of strength and of weakness. He was the ablest polemic this country has ever produced. His command of strong, idiomatic, controversial English was unrivaled. His faculty of lucid statement and compact reasoning has never been surpassed. Without the graces of fancy or the arts of rhetoric, he was incomparable in direct, pungent, forceful discussion. A keen observer and an omnivorous reader, he had acquired an immense fund of varied knowledge, and he marshaled facts with singular skill and aptness.

In an era remarkable for strong editors in the New York press—embracing Raymond of the "Times," the elder Bennett of the "Herald," Watson Webb of the "Courier-Enquirer," William Cullen Bryant of the "Evening Post," with Thurlow Weed and Edwin Crosswell in the rival journals at Albany—Mr. Greeley easily surpassed them all. His mind was original, creative, incessantly active. His industry was as unwearying as his fertility was inexhaustible. Great as was his intellectual power, his chief strength came from the depth and earnestness of his moral convictions. In the long and arduous battle against the aggressions of slavery, he had been sleepless and untiring in rousing and quickening the public conscience. He was keenly alive to the distinctions of right and wrong, and his philanthropy responded to every call of humanity. His sympathies were equally touched by the sufferings of the famine-stricken Irish and by the wrongs of the plundered Indians.

Next to Henry Clay, whose ardent disciple he was, he had done more than any other man to educate his countrymen in the American system of protection to home industry. He had on all occasions zealously defended the rights of labor; he had waged unsparing war on the evils of intemperance; he had made himself an oracle with the American farmers; and his influence was even more potent in the remote prairie homes than within the shadow of Printing-House Square. With his dogmatic earnestness, his extraordinary mental qualities, his moral power, and his quick sympathy with the instincts and impulses of the masses, he was in a peculiar sense the Tribune of the people. In any reckoning of the personal forces of the century, Horace Greeley must be counted among the foremost—intellectually and morally.

When he left the fields of labor in which he had become illustrious, to pass the ordeal of a Presidential candidate, the opposite and weaker sides of his character and career were brought into view. He was headstrong, impulsive and opinionated. If he had the strength of a giant in battle, he lacked the wisdom of the sage in council. If he was irresistible in his own appropriate sphere of moral and economic discussion, he was uncertain and unstable when he ventured beyond its limits. He was a powerful agitator and a matchless leader of debate, rather than a master of government.

Those who most admired his honesty, courage and power in the realm of his true greatness, most distrusted his fitness to hold the reins of administration. He had in critical periods evinced a want both of firmness and of sagacity. When the Southern States were on the eve of secession and the temper of the country was on trial, he had, though with honest intentions, shown signs of irresolution and vacillation. When he was betrayed into the ill-advised and abortive peace negotiations with Southern commissioners at Niagara, he had displayed the lack of tact and penetration which made the people doubt the solidity and coolness of his judgment. His method of dealing with the most intricate problems of finance seemed experimental and rash. The sensitive interests of business shrank from his visionary theories and his dangerous empiricism. His earlier affiliation with novel and doubtful social schemes had laid him open to the reproach of being called a man of isms.

Mr. Greeley had moreover weakened himself by showing a singular thirst for public office. It is strange that one who held a commanding station, and who wielded an unequaled influence, should have been ambitious for the smaller honors of public life. But Mr. Greeley had craved even minor offices, from which he could have derived no distinction, and, in his own phrase, had dissolved the firm of Seward, Weed and Greeley because, as he conceived, his claims to official promotion was not fairly recognized. This known aspiration added to the reasons which discredited his unnatural alliance with the Democracy. His personal characteristics, always marked, were exaggerated and distorted in the portraitures drawn by his adversaries. All adverse considerations were brought to bear with irresistible effect as the canvass proceeded, and his splendid services and undeniable greatness could not weigh in the scale against the political elements and personal disqualifications with which his Presidential candidacy was identified.

The political agitation became general in the country as early as July. Senator Conkling inaugurated the Grant campaign in New York with an elaborate and comprehensive review of the personal and public issues on trial. Senator Sherman and other leading speakers took the field with equal promptness. On the opposite side, Senator Sumner, who had sought in May to challenge and prevent the renomination of General Grant by concentrating in one massive broadside all that could be suggested against him, now appeared in a public letter advising the colored people to vote for Greeley. Mr. Blaine replied in a letter pointing out that Mr. Greeley, in denying the power of the General Government to interpose, had committed himself to a policy which left the colored people without protection.

The September elections had ordinarily given the earliest indication in Presidential campaigns; but circumstances conspired this year to make the North Carolina election, which was held on the 1st of August, the preliminary test of popular feeling. The earliest returns from North Carolina, coming from the eastern part of the State, were favorable to the partisans of Mr. Greeley. They claimed a decided victory, and were highly elated. The returns from the western and mountain counties, which were not all received for several days, reversed the first reports, and established a Republican success.

This change produced a reaction, and set the tide in the opposite direction. From this hour the popular current was clearly with the Republicans. The September elections in Vermont and Maine resulted in more than the average Republican majorities, and demonstrated that Mr. Greeley's candidacy had not broken the lines of the party. Early in that month a body of Democrats, who declined to accept Mr. Greeley, and who called themselves "Straightouts," held a convention at Louisville, and nominated Charles O'Connor for President and John Quincy Adams for Vice-President. The ticket received a small number of votes in many States, but did not become an important factor in the national struggle.

In anticipation of the October elections Mr. Greeley made an extended tour through Pennsylvania, Ohio and Indiana, addressing great masses of people every day and many times a day during a period of two weeks. His speeches, while chiefly devoted to his view of the duty and policy of pacification, discussed many questions and many phases of the chief question. They were varied, forcible and well considered. They presented his case with an ability which could not be exceeded, and they added to the general estimate of his intellectual faculties and resources. He called out a larger proportion of those who intended to vote against him than any candidate had ever before succeeded in doing. His name had been honored for so many years in every Republican household that the desire to see and hear him was universal, and secured to him the majesty of numbers at every meeting. So great indeed was the general demonstration of interest that a degree of uneasiness was created at Republican headquarters as to the ultimate effect of his tour.

The State contests had been strongly organized on both sides at the decisive points. In New York the Democrats nominated Francis Kernan for Governor—a man of spotless character and great popularity. The Republicans selected General John A. Dix as the rival candidate, on the earnest suggestion of Thurlow Weed, whose sagacity in regard to the strength of political leaders was rarely at fault. General Dix was in his seventy-fifth year, but was fresh and vigorous both in body and mind. In Indiana the leading Democrat, Thomas A. Hendricks, accepted the gubernatorial nomination and the leadership of his party against General Thomas M. Browne, a popular Republican and a strong man on the stump. Pennsylvania was the scene of a peculiarly bitter and angry conflict. General Hartranft, the Republican candidate for Governor, had been Auditor-General of the State, and his administration of the office was bitterly assailed. The old factional differences in the State now entered into the antagonism, and he was strenuously fought by an element of his own party under the inspiration of Colonel Forney, who, while professedly supporting Grant, threw all the force of the Philadelphia "Press" into the warfare against Hartranft.

This violent opposition encouraged the partisans of Mr. Greeley with the hope that they might secure the prestige of victory over the Republicans in Pennsylvania, whose October verdicts had always proved an unerring index to presidential elections. But they were doomed to disappointment. The people saw that the charges against General Hartranft were not only unfounded but malicious, and he was chosen Governor by more than 35,000 majority. Ohio gave a Republican majority on the same day of more than 14,000; and though Mr. Hendricks carried Indiana by 1,148, this narrow margin for the strongest Democrat in the State was accepted as confirming the sure indications in the other States.

The defeat of Mr. Greeley and the reëlection of General Grant were now, in the popular belief, assured. The result was the most decisive, in the popular vote, of any Presidential election since the unopposed choice of Monroe in 1820; and on the electoral vote the only contests so one-sided were in the election of Pierce in 1852, and the second election of Lincoln in 1864, when the States in rebellion did not participate. The majorities were unprecedented. General Grant carried Pennsylvania by 137,548, New York by 53,455, Illinois by 57,006, Iowa by 60,370, Massachusetts by 74,212, Michigan by

THE GREELEY CAMPAIGN 151

60,100, Ohio by 37,501, and Indiana by 22,515. Several of the Southern States presented figures of similar proportion. . . .

The political disaster to Mr. Greeley was followed by a startling and melancholy conclusion. He was called during the last days of the canvass to the bedside of his dying wife, whom he buried before the day of election. Despite this sorrow and despite the defeat, which, in separating him from his old associates, was more than an ordinary political reverse, he promptly returned with unshaken resolve and intrepid spirit to the editorship of the "Tribune"—the true sphere of his influence, the field of his real conquests. But the strain through which he had passed, following years of incessant care and labor, had broken his vigorous constitution. His physical strength was completely undermined, his superb intellectual powers gave way. Before the expiration of the month which witnessed his crushing defeat he had gone to his rest. The controversies which had so recently divided the country were hushed in the presence of death; and all the people, remembering only his noble impulses, his great work for humanity, his broad impress upon the age, united in honoring and mourning one of the most remarkable men in American history.

CARPET-BAG GOVERNMENT

By James Shepherd Pike

THIS is one of a series of articles Pike wrote after visiting South Carolina in 1873, and observing the evils of carpet-bag government. They were published by D. Appleton & Company as "The Prostrate State: South Carolina Under Negro Government." Before the Civil War the author was Washington correspondent of the New York Tribune. During the war he was American Minister to the Netherlands. In the Grant-Greeley campaign of 1873 he supported the Liberal Republican movement in opposing further coercive measures in the Southern States.

During this orgy of misgovernment in the South a wholesale system of plunder was inaugurated. In South Carolina alone the public debt was increased from $5,000,000 in 1868 to $18,000,000 in 1872, with little to show for it. The tax levy of $500,000 a year were raised to $2,000,000, although the value of taxable property was reduced one-half.

IN the place of an old aristocratic society stands the rude form of the most ignorant democracy that mankind ever saw, invested with the functions of government. It is the dregs of the population habilitated in the robes of their intelligent predecessors, and asserting over them the rule of ignorance and corruption, through the inexorable machinery of a majority of numbers. It is barbarism overwhelming civilization by physical force. It is the slave rioting in the halls of his master, and putting that master under his feet. And, though it is done without malice and without vengeance, it is nevertheless none the less completely and absolutely done. Let us approach nearer and take a closer view.

CARPET-BAG GOVERNMENT

We will enter the House of Representatives. Here sit one hundred and twenty-four members. Of these, twenty-three are white men, representing the remains of the old civilization. . . . Deducting the twenty-three members referred to, who comprise the entire strength of the opposition, we find one hundred and one remaining. Of this one hundred and one, ninety-four are colored, and seven are their white allies. Thus the blacks outnumber the whole body of whites in the House more than three to one. . . . As things stand, the body is almost literally a Black Parliament, and it is the only one on the face of the earth which is the representative of a white constituency and the professed exponent of an advanced type of modern civilization. But the reader will find almost any portraiture inadequate to give a vivid idea of the body, and enable him to comprehend the complete metamorphosis of the South Carolina Legislature, without observing its details. The Speaker is black, the Clerk is black, the doorkeepers are black, the little pages are black, the chairman of the Ways and Means is black, and the chaplain is coal-black. At some of the desks sit colored men whose types it would be hard to find outside of Congo; whose costume, visages, attitudes and expression, only befit the forecastle of a buccaneer. It must be remembered, also, that these men, with not more than half a dozen exceptions, have been themselves slaves, and that their ancestors were slaves for generations. . . .

The corruption of the State government of South Carolina is a topic that has grown threadbare in the handling. The last administration stole right hand and left with a recklessness and audacity without parallel. The robbers under it embraced all grades of people. The thieves had to combine to aid one another. It took a combination of the principal authorities to get at the Treasury, and they had to share the plunder alike. All the smaller fry had their proportions, the legislators and lobbymen included. The principal men of the Scott administration are living in Columbia, and nobody undertakes to call them to account. They do not attempt even to conceal their plunder. If everybody was not implicated in the robberies of the Treasury, some way would be found to bring them to light. All that people know is that the State bonded debt had been increased from five to fifteen millions, and that, besides this, there are all sorts of current obligations to pay afloat, issued by State officers who had authority to bind the Treasury. They are all tinctured with fraud, and some of them are such scandalous swindles that the courts have been able temporarily to stop their payment.

The whole of the late administration, which terminated its existence in November, 1872, was a morass of rottenness, and the present administration was born of the corruptions of that; but for the exhaustion of the State, there is no good reason to believe it would steal less than its predecessor. There seems to be no hope, therefore, that the villainies of the past will be speedily uncovered. The present Governor was Speaker of the last House, and he is credited with having issued during his term in office over $400,000 of pay "certificates" which are still unredeemed and for which there is no appropriation, but which must be saddled on the taxpayers sooner or later. . . .

. . . Then it has been found that some of the most unscrupulous white and black robbers who have, as members or lobbyists, long plied their nefarious trade at the capital, still disfigure and disgrace the present Assembly. So tainted is the atmosphere with corruption, so universally implicated is everybody about the government, of such a character are the ornaments of society at the capital, that there is no such thing as an influential local opinion to be brought against the scamps. They plunder, and glory in it. They steal, and defy you to prove it. The legalization of fraudulent scrip is regarded simply as a smart operation. The purchase of a senatorship is considered only a profitable trade. Those who make the most out of the operation are the best fellows. "How did you get your money?" was asked of a prominent legislator and lobbyist. "I stole it," was the prompt reply. The same man pursues his trade today, openly and unabashed. A leading member of the last administration was told he had the credit of having robbed the State of his large fortune. "Let them prove it," was his only answer. Meanwhile both of them openly revel in their riches under the very shadow of the lean and hungry Treasury whence their ill-gotten gains were filched.

As has been already said, it is believed that the lank impoverishment of the Treasury and the total abasement and destruction of the State credit alone prevent the continuance of robbery on the old scale. As it is, taxation is not in the least diminished, and nearly two millions per annum are raised for State expenses where $400,000 formerly sufficed. This affords succulent pasturage for a large crowd. For it must be remembered that not a dollar of it goes for interest on the State debt. The barter and sale of the offices in which the finances of the State are manipulated, which are divided among the numerous small counties under a system offering unusual facilities for the business, go on with as much activity as ever. The new Governor has the reputation of spending $30,000 or $40,000 a year on a salary of $3,500, but his financial operations are taken as a matter of course, and only referred to with a slight shrug of the shoulders.

. . . The narration I have given sufficiently shows how things have gone and are going in this State, but its effect would be much heightened if there were time and room for details. Here is one: The total amount of the stationery bill of the House for the twenty years preceding 1861 averaged $400 per annum. Last year it was $16,000. . . . The influence of a free press is well understood in South Carolina. It was understood and dreaded under the old régime, and was muzzled accordingly. Nearly all the newspapers in the State are now subsidized. The State government employs and pays them "ad libitum." One installment of $75,000 lately went to about twenty-five papers in sums ranging from $1,000 to $7,000 apiece, a list of which was published by order of a vote of the Legislature a short time ago. Down here these small weekly sheets can be pretty nearly kept going on these subsidies. Of course none of the deviltry of the State government is likely to be exposed through them. The whole amount of the printing bills of the State last year, it is computed (for every thing here has to be in part guesswork), aggregated the immense sum of $600,000. . . .

The black men who led the colored forces the other day against a railroad charter, because their votes had not been purchased, were models of hardihood in legislative immorality. They were not so wily nor so expert, perhaps, as the one white man who was their ally in debate, but who dodged the vote from fear of his constituency; but they exhibited on that, as they have on other occasions, an entire want of moral tone, and a brazen effrontery in pursuing their venal purposes that could not be surpassed by the most accomplished "striker" of Tweed's old gang. I have before alluded to the fact that on this occasion the blacks voted alone, not one white man going with them in opposing the measure they had conspired to defeat in order to extort money from the corporators.

This mass of black representatives, however ignorant in other respects, were here seen to be well schooled in the arts of corruption. They knew precisely what they were about and just what they wanted, and they knew the same when they voted for Patterson for Senator.

This is the kind of moral education the ignorant blacks of the State are getting by being made legislators. The first lessons were, to be sure, given by whites from abroad. But the success of the carpet-baggers has stimulated the growth of knavish native demagogues, who bid fair to surpass their instructors. The imitative powers of the blacks and their destitution of morale put them already in the front ranks of the men who are robbing and disgracing the State, and cheating the gallows of its due.

THE PANIC OF 1873

By E. Benjamin Andrews

DR. ANDREWS, from whose "History of the Last Quarter-Century of the United States," this account is taken, by permission of Charles Scribner's Sons, occupied the chair of political economy and finance in Cornell University, 1888-9, and was president of Brown University from 1889 to 1898. He resigned because of criticism by the university trustees of his advocacy of free silver. In 1892 he was a United States commissioner to the Brussels monetary conference, and was a strong advocate of international bimetallism.

The crisis of 1873 is usually dated from the failure of Jay Cooke & Company. There had been premonitory symptoms of the approaching collapse. Railroad-building reached its highest point in 1871, pig-iron its highest price in 1872. The crisis lasted a few months only, but was followed by a tenaciously long period of depression, the lowest point of which was touched in 1876.

THE panic of 1873, so far as it resulted from contraction, had its main origin abroad, not in America, so that its subordinate causes were generally looked upon as its sole occasion; yet these bye causes were important. The shocking destruction of wealth by fires and by reckless speculation, of course, had a baneful effect. During 1872 the balance of trade was strongly against the United States. The circulation of depreciated paper money had brought to many an apparent prosperity which was not real, leading to the free creation of debts by individuals, corporations, towns, cities and States. An unprecedented mileage of railways had been constructed. Much supposed wealth consisted in the bonds of these railroads and of other new concerns, like mining and manufacturing corporations. Thus the entire business of the country was on a basis of inflation, and when contraction came disaster was inevitable.

In the course of the summer solid values began to be hoarded and interest rates consequently to rise. In August there was a partial corner in gold, broken by a government sale of $6,000,000. In September panic came, with suspension of several large banking-houses in New York. Jay Cooke & Co., who had invested heavily in the construction of the Northern Pacific Railway, suspended on September 18th. When authoritative news of this event was made known in the Stock Exchange a perfect stampede of the brokers ensued. They surged out of the Exchange, tumbling pell-mell over each other in the general confusion, hastening to notify their respective houses. Next day, September 19th, Fiske & Hatch, very conservative people, went down.

September 19th was a second Black Friday. Never since the original Black Friday had the Street and the Stock Exchange been so frantic. The weather, dark and rainy, seemed to sympathize with the gloom which clouded the financial situation. Wall, Broad and Nassau Streets were thronged with people. From the corner of Wall Street and Broadway down to the corner of Hanover Street a solid mass of men filled both sidewalks. From the post-office along Nassau Street down Broad Street to Exchange Place another dense throng moved slowly, aimlessly, hither and thither. Sections of Broadway itself were packed. Weaving in and out like the shuttles in a loom were brokers and brokers' clerks making the best speed they could from point to point. All faces wore a bewildered and foreboding look. To help them seem cool, moneyed men talked about the weather, but their incoherent words and nervous motions betrayed their anxiety. The part of Wall Street at the corner of Broad Street held a specially interested mass of men. They seemed like an assemblage anxiously awaiting the appearance of a great spectacle. High up on the stone balustrade of the Sub-Treasury were numerous spectators, umbrellas sheltering them from the pelting rain as they gazed with rapt attention on the scene below. All the brokers' offices were filled. In each, at the first click of the indicator, everybody present was breathless, showing an interest more and more intense as the figures telegraphed were read off.

It was half-past ten in the morning when the Fiske & Hatch failure was announced in the Stock Exchange. For a moment there was silence; then a hoarse murmur broke out from bulls and bears alike, followed by yells and cries indescribable, clearly audible on the street. Even the heartless bear, in glee over the havoc he was making, paused to utter a growl of sorrow that gentlemen so honorable should become ursine prey. The news of the failure ran like a prairie fire, spreading dismay that showed itself on all faces. Annotators of values in the various offices made known in doleful ticks the depreciation of stocks and securities. Old habitués of the exchanges, each usually placid as a moonlit lake, were wrought up till they acted like wild men.

At the corner of Broad Street and Exchange Place a delirious crowd of money-lenders and borrowers collected and tried to fix a rate for loans. The matter hung in the balance for some time until the extent of the panic became known. They bid until the price of money touched one-half of one per cent. a day and legal interest. One man, after lending $30,000 at three-eighths per cent., said that he had $20,000 left, but that he thought he would not lend it. As he said this he turned toward his office, but was immediately surrounded by about twenty borrowers who hung on to his arms till he had agreed to lend the $20,000.

The Stock Exchange witnessed the chief tragedy and the chief farce of the day. Such tumult, push and bellowing had never been known there even in the wildest moments of the war. The interior of the Exchange was of noble altitude, with a vaulted top, brilliantly colored in Renaissance design that sprang upward with a strength and grace seldom so happily united. A cluster of gas-jets, hanging high, well illuminated the enclosure. On the capacious floor, unobstructed by pillars or by furniture, save one small table whereon a large basket of flowers rested, a mob of brokers and brokers' clerks surged back and forth, filling the immense space above with roars and screams. The floor was portioned off to some twenty

THE PANIC OF 1873

different groups. Here was one tossing "New York Central" up and down; near by another playing ball with "Wabash"; "Northwestern" jumped and sank as if afflicted with St. Vitus's dance. In the middle of the floor "Rock Island" cut up similar capers. In a remote corner "Pacific Mail" was beaten with clubs, while "Harlem" rose like a balloon filled with pure hydrogen. The uninitiated expected every instant to see the mob fight. Jobbers squared off at each other and screamed and yelled violently, flinging their arms around and producing a scene which Bedlam itself could not equal.

Behind the raised desk, in snowy shirt-front and necktie, stood the president of the Exchange, his strong tenor voice every now and then ringing out over the Babel of sounds beneath. The gallery opposite him contained an eager throng of spectators bending forward and craning their necks to view the pandemonium on the floor. The rush for this gallery was fearful, and apparently, but for the utmost effort of the police, must have proved fatal to some. Excitement in Wall Street not infrequently drew crowds to the main front of the Exchange; but hardly ever, if ever before, had the vicinity been so packed as now. Two large blackboards exhibited in chalk figures the incessantly fluctuating quotations. Telegraph wires connected the Exchange with a thousand indicators throughout the city, whence the quotations, big with meaning to many, were flashed over the land.

THE PANIC OF 1873

The first Black Friday was a bull Friday; the second was a bear Friday. Early in the panic powerful brokers began to sell short, and they succeeded in hammering down from ten to forty per cent. many of the finest stocks like "New York Central," "Erie," "Wabash," "Northwestern," "Rock Island," and "Western Union." They then bought to cover their sales. Bull brokers, unable to pay their contracts, shrieked for margin money, which their principals would not or could not put up. They also sought relief from the banks, but in vain. It had long been the practice of certain banks, though contrary to law, early each day to certify checks to enormous amounts in favor of brokers who had not a cent on deposit to their credit, the understanding in each case being that before three o'clock the broker would hand in enough cash or securities to cancel his debt. The banks now refused this accommodation. In the Exchange, eighteen names were read off of brokers who could not fulfil their contracts. As fast as the failures were announced the news was carried out on the street. In spite of the rain hundreds of people gathered about the offices of fallen reputation, and gazed curiously through the windows, trying to make out how the broken brokers were behaving. Toward evening, as the clouds lifted over Trinity spire, showing a ruddy flush in the west, everybody, save some reluctant bears, said, "The worst is over," and breathed a sigh of relief. The crowd melted, one by one the tiny little Broadway coupés rattled off, one by

THE PANIC OF 1873

one the newsboys ceased shrieking, and night closed over the wet street.

In deference to a general wish that dealings in stocks should cease, the Exchange was shut on Saturday, September 20th, and not opened again till the 30th. Such closure had never occurred before. On Sunday morning President Grant and Secretary Richardson, of the Treasury, came to New York, spending the day in anxious consultation with Vanderbilt, Clews, and other prominent business men.

Had the Secretary of the Treasury acted promptly and firmly he might have relieved the situation much; but he vacillated. Some $13,500,000 in five-twenty bonds were bought, and a few millions of the greenbacks which Secretary McCulloch had called in for cancellation were set free. But as Mr. Richardson announced no policy on which the public could depend, most of the cash let loose was instantly hoarded in vaults or used in the purchase of other bonds then temporarily depressed, so doing nothing whatever to allay the distress. On the 25th the Treasury ceased buying bonds. The person who, at the worst, sustained the market and kept it from breaking to a point where half of the street would have been inevitably ruined, was Jay Gould, mischief itself on the first Black Friday, but on this one a blessing. He bought during the low prices several hundred thousand shares of railroad stocks, principally of the Vanderbilt stripe, and in this way put a check on the ruinous decline.

The national banks of New York weathered this cyclone by a novel device of the Clearing-house or associated banks. They pooled their cash and collaterals into a common fund, placed this in the hands of a trusty committee, and issued against it loan certificates that were receivable at the Clearing-house, just like cash, in payment of debit balances. Ten million dollars' worth of these certificates was issued at first, a sum subsequently doubled. This Clearing-house paper served its purpose admirably. By October 3d confidence was so restored that $1,000,000 of it was called in and canceled, followed next day by $1,500,000 more. None of it was long outstanding. The Clearing-house febrifuge was successfully applied also in Boston, Philadelphia, Pittsburgh and other cities, but not in Chicago.

The panic overspread the country. Credit in business was refused, debtors were pressed for payment, securities were rushed into the markets and fell greatly in price. Even United States bonds went down from five to ten per cent. There was a run upon savings-banks, many of which succumbed. Manufactured goods were little salable, and the prices of agricultural products painfully sank. Factories began to run on short time, many closed entirely, many corporations failed. The peculiarity of this crisis was the slowness with which it abated, though fortunately its acute phase was of brief duration. No date could be set as its term, its evil effects dragging on through years.

CUBAN INTERVENTION PROPOSED

By Hamilton Fish, Secretary of State

HAMILTON FISH was Secretary of State in Grant's Cabinet when he sent this official communication to Caleb Cushing, United States Minister to Spain. That was in 1875 and his firm stand brought about a satisfactory settlement of the complications arising in the Virginius affair, and resulted in the postponement of a war with Spain until 1898.

Diplomatic negotiations with Spain over Cuba began soon after the United States had acknowledged the independence of the South and Central American countries that had thrown off the Spanish yoke. The Cuban insurrection had been in progress for seven years when this document was drafted.

On October 31, 1873, the Virginius, an American vessel carrying arms and men to the aid of the Cuban insurgents, had been captured by a Spanish warship, and her captain, with 36 of the crew and 16 passengers, were executed.

AT the time of your departure for Madrid, apart from the general question of the unsatisfactory condition of affairs in Cuba and the failure to suppress the revolution, several prominent questions remained unadjusted, the settlement of which was deemed necessary before any satisfactory relations with Spain could be established or maintained. Upon all of these you were instructed.

The most prominent among them were the questions arising from the embargo and confiscation of estates of American citizens in Cuba; those relating to the trial of American citizens in that island, in violation of treaty obligations, and the claims arising out of the capture of the "Virginius," including the trial and punishment of General Burriel.

After the expiration of more than eighteen months, it seems advisable to examine what progress has been made and to consider our present relations with Spain. . . .

. . . the promises made and repeated, the assurances given from time to time that something should be done, the admission of the justice of the demands of this country, at least to the extent of expressing regret for these wrongs and promising redress, followed as they have been by absolutely no performance and no practical steps whatever towards performance, need no extended comment.

In the cases of embargo and confiscation, not only have wrongs been long since done, but continuing and repeated wrongs are daily inflicted. The authorities of Spain in Cuba, during all this time, have been and are using the revenues of the confiscated or embargoed estates, appropriating much of the property itself, and in some cases executing long leases, or actually making sales, either on the allegation that taxes were due, or without any excuse whatever.

Turning to the questions which arose from the capture of the "Virginius," and the execution which followed, no extended reference is required.

The particulars of the delivery of the vessel to this Government, and the payment to both Great Britain and the United States of considerable sums as compensation for the acts of the authorities in ordering the execution of fifty-three of the passengers and crew under circumstances of peculiar brutality, have passed into history.

So far as a payment of money can atone for the execution of these unprotected prisoners, that has been accomplished.

The higher and more imperative duty which the government of Spain assumed by the protocol of November 29, 1873, namely, to bring to justice General Burriel and the other principal offenders in this tragedy, has been evaded and entirely neglected. . . .

Having touched on these particular questions which have lately been prominent as disturbing causes with Spain, it is necessary to also refer to the general condition of affairs in Cuba as affecting our relations with the mother country.

In my No. 2, of February 6, 1874, (the first instruction addressed to you on general matters pertaining to your mission,) I referred at length to the views entertained by the President and to the position of this Government.

It was then more than five years since an organized insurrection had broken out which the government of Spain had been entirely unable to suppress. . . .

Almost two years have passed since those instructions were issued . . . and it would appear that the situation has in no respect improved.

The horrors of war have in no perceptible measure abated; the inconveniences and injuries which we then suffered have remained, and others have been added; the ravages of war have touched new parts of the island, and well-nigh ruined its financial and agricultural system and its relations to the commerce of the world. No effective steps have been taken to establish reforms or remedy abuses, and the effort to suppress the insurrection, by force alone, has been a complete failure. . . .

The United States purchases more largely than any other people of the productions of the island of Cuba, and therefore, more than any other for this reason, and still more by reason of its immediate neighborhood, is interested in the arrest of a system of wanton destruction which disgraces the age and affects every commercial people on the face of the globe.

Under these circumstances, and in view of the fact that Spain has rejected all suggestions of reform or offers of mediation made by this Government, and has refused all measures looking to a reconciliation, except on terms which make reconciliation an impossibility, the difficulty of the situation becomes increased.

When, however, in addition to these general causes of difficulty, we find the Spanish government neglectful also of the obligations of treaties and solemn compacts, and unwilling to afford any redress for long-continued and well-founded wrongs suffered by our citizens, it becomes a serious question how long such a condition of things can or should be allowed to exist, and compels us to inquire whether the point has not been reached where longer endurance ceases to be possible.

During all this time, and under these aggravated circumstances, this Government has not failed to perform her obligations to Spain as scrupulously as toward other nations. In fact, it might be said that we have not only been long suffering, because of the embarrassments surrounding the Spanish government, but particularly careful to give no occasion for complaint for the same reason.

I regret to say that the authorities of Spain have not at all times appreciated our intentions or our purposes in these respects, and, while insisting that a state of war does not exist in Cuba, and that no rights as belligerents should be accorded to the insurrectionists, have at the same time demanded for themselves all the rights and privileges which flow from actual and acknowledged war.

It will be apparent that such a state of things cannot continue. It is absolutely necessary to the maintenance of our relations with Spain, even on their present footing, that our just demands for the return to citizens of the United States of their estates in Cuba, unincumbered, and for securing to them a trial for offenses according to treaty provisions and all other rights guaranteed by treaty and by public law, should be complied with. . . .

Moreover, apart from these particular questions, in the opinion of the President, the time has arrived when the interests of this country, the preservation of its commerce, and the instincts of humanity alike demand that some speedy and satisfactory ending be made of the strife that is devastating Cuba. . . .

The contest and disorder in Cuba affect the United States directly and injuriously by the presence in this country of partisans of the revolt who have fled hither (in consequence of the proximity of territory) as to a political asylum, and who, by their plottings, are disturbers of the public peace.

The United States has exerted itself to the utmost, for seven years, to repress unlawful acts on the part of these self-exiled subjects of Spain, relying on the promise of Spain to pacify the island. Seven years of strain on the powers of this Government to fulfill all that the most exacting demands of one government can make, under any doctrine or claim of international obligation, upon another, have not witnessed the much hoped-for pacification. The United States feels itself entitled to be relieved of this strain.

The severe measures, injurious to the United States and often in conflict with public law, which the colonial officers have taken to subdue the insurrection; the indifference, and ofttimes the offensive assaults upon the just susceptibilities of the people of the United States and their Government, which have characterized that portion of the peninsular population of Havana which has sustained and upheld, if it has not controlled, successive governors-general, and which have led to the disregard of orders and decrees which the more enlarged wisdom and the more friendly councils of the home government had enacted; the cruelty and inhumanity which have characterized the contest, both on the part of the colonial government and of the revolt, for seven years, and the destruction of valuable properties and industries by arson and pillage, which Spain appears unable, however desirous, to prevent and stop, in an island three thousand miles distant from her shores, but lying within sight of our coast, with which trade and constant intercourse are unavoidable, are causes of annoyance and of injury to the United States, which a people cannot be expected to tolerate without the assured prospect of their termination.

The United States has more than once been solicited by the insurgents to extend to them its aid, but has for years hitherto resisted such solicitation, and has endeavored by the tender of its good offices, in the way of mediation, advice, and remonstrance, to bring to an end a great evil, which has pressed sorely upon the interests both of the Government and of the people of the United States, as also upon the commercial interests of other nations. . . .

The President hopes that Spain may spontaneously adopt measures looking to a reconciliation, and to the speedy restoration of peace, and the organization of a stable and satisfactory system of government in the island of Cuba.

In the absence of any prospect of a termination of the war, or of any change in the manner in which it has been conducted on either side, he feels that the time is at hand when it may be the duty of other governments to intervene, solely with the view of bringing to an end a disastrous and destructive conflict, and of restoring peace in the island of Cuba. No government is more deeply interested in the order and peaceful administration of this island than is that of the United States, and none has suffered as has the United States from the condition which has obtained there during the past six or seven years. He will, therefore, feel it his duty at an early day to submit the subject in this light, and accompanied by an expression of the views above presented, for the consideration of Congress. . . .

It is believed to be a just and friendly act to frankly communicate this conclusion to the Spanish government.

You will, therefore, take an early occasion thus to inform that government.

THE CENTENNIAL OF THE REPUBLIC

A Contemporary Account

NO EVENT of the reconstruction period following the Civil War compared in importance with the Centennial Exposition held in Philadelphia from May 10 to November 10, 1876. Being the first exhibition of the kind in the United States, it paved the way for subsequent undertakings such as the World's Fair at Chicago and the Louisiana Exposition at St. Louis.

Despite the panic of 1873 and the three years of depression that followed, the success of the project was unprecedented. To the outside world it was a revelation of the economic power and progress of the hundred-year-old Republic. It was significant that of the forty-nine foreign governments represented among the exhibitors, the magnitude of the British exhibit was only exceeded by our own. At this exposition articles of Japanese manufacture first became well known in the United States.

AN exposition of the industry of all nations, to be held in the United States, was suggested by similar fairs which have been held within the last twenty years—in London, Paris and Vienna. The holding of it in 1876 was suggested by the fact that during this year the Republic completes its hundredth year of existence. It therefore seemed fitting that, while each community might celebrate by itself the Fourth of July of this year with special éclat, and where there had been battles or Revolutionary events might celebrate them also with pomp and circumstance, the nation as a whole should this year make one grand jubilee, and out of its unparalleled prosperity exhibit its advance, and invite the whole world to be present. Several parties undertook to inaugurate it, and several places were suggested as its seat—Washington, New York and Philadelphia. The latter place was finally selected on account of its central location, its facilities of access, its ability to provide for a multitude, and to carry them about the city, and its ample and convenient space in Fairmount Park for the purposes contemplated, and also on account of its numerous and marked Revolutionary memories.

The General Government was petitioned to aid the enterprise pecuniarily, and by an exhibit, and by its countenance make it an international affair, becoming the medium of invitation to foreign countries to participate. The Government complied. Philadelphia, Pennsylvania, several other States, and numerous individuals in New York City and elsewhere subscribed liberally to the project. The Park Commissioners set apart 450 acres on which to locate the fair, 236 of which have been enclosed and applied. July the fourth, 1874, ground was first broken for the enterprise. May the tenth, 1876, though not quite completed, but being sufficiently so, it was opened by the President of the United States, accompanied by suitable ceremonies, military and civic, of music and of speech, and in the presence of numerous dignitaries, home and foreign, and of the people. As many as 250,000 people, it was estimated, were on the grounds that day. The Exhibition is to be kept open until November the tenth. On opening day, the President of the United States and the Emperor of Brazil started the Corliss engine, which runs the machinery in Machinery Hall. Of this act Bayard Taylor observes, "North and South America started the machinery of the world." . . .

There are nearly two hundred buildings on the grounds, all of them erected within two years. Some of them are to remain. But most of them are to be taken down at the close of the Fair. Some of these buildings are very large. Others are splendid, substantial, costly. All of them are an ornament, useful, creditable and a study. From sixty to seventy acres are under roof. These buildings are arranged chiefly on fine Avenues—the Avenue of the Republic, Belmont, Fountain, Agriculture and State avenues.

The Main Exhibition Building is 1,880 feet long, 464 feet wide, and 70 feet high. It has corner towers 75 feet, and central towers 120 feet high. It is built of iron and glass, and cost over $1,500,000. Over 5,000,000 pounds of iron have been used in constructing the roof, trusses and girders. It covers $21\frac{1}{2}$ acres, and is the largest building in the world. There are four entrances, one on each side and end. Within are twelve miles of show. Over thirty countries, including nearly all the civilized nations of the globe, here exhibit themselves and their industries. The United States exhibit covers about seven acres, or nearly one-third. Great Britain and her dependencies come next, occupying about one-fifth of the space. Here is to be seen almost every thing that the globe, through the industry and skill of its men, produces, except what is peculiar to the other buildings. Here are things rare, ancient, costly and curious, and in endless variety. A pair of vases valued at $3,000 are here. Though the building is so spacious, it has been found necessary to attach three annexes. Gilmore's band of sixty-five performers, gives two concerts daily, free, in this edifice.

Machinery Hall covers 13 acres. A Corliss Engine of 1,400 horse power, runs the machinery through over two miles of shafting. There are 1,500 sections, and several thousand machines in this building. Here is a waterfall 36 feet wide, 33 feet deep, and four inches thick, carrying 30,000 gallons per minute. On the outside of the main front of this building is a clock; and in the towers a chime of bells, for which Professor Widdows, the Director, has arranged a great many popular airs. Connected with this building, are as many as eleven annexes.

Agricultural Hall covers 10 acres. There are five annexes to this building. One of these is the Pomological, where will be displayed fruits and vegetables in their season. It covers two acres. A stock yard is also connected, which is near the Belmont station of the Pennsylvania Railroad; where is an Ox of 4,000 pound weight, and a Heifer of 3,300. In the main building is an Aquaria, and Professor Ward of Rochester, has a rare exhibit in Paleontology. Brazil displays one thousand varieties of wood. There are three hundred plows here; one, it is said, cost $1,000. Many wonderful labor-saving inventions are here exhibited, in which it is probable the United States takes the lead.

Memorial Hall or the Fine Arts Building is one of the most costly on the grounds. Its cost is set down as $1,125,000. It is built of granite, iron and glass. It is 365 feet long, 210 feet wide, and 59 feet high, surmounted by a dome 150 feet high, with a figure of Columbia on the top, and at the base colossal figures typifying the four quarters of the globe. Here are exhibited paintings and statuary. It affords 75,000 feet of wall space for the former, and 20,000 feet of floor space for the latter. It is intended to remain after the Exhibition is over, and will probably be the seat of a museum, &c., similar somewhat to the Kensington Gardens, London. There are two annexes to this building.

Horticultural Hall is the last to be mentioned of the main buildings which have been erected by the Commission. Here are exhibited tropical and other plants. Orange and lemon trees, banana, sago and like trees, are here to be seen. Also a century plant ready to bloom. Around are thirty-five acres of garden. This building also is intended to be permanent.

Another great building is the one erected by the United States Government. With the grounds attached it covers seven acres. Congress appropriated over $500,000 for the erection of the building and its exhibit. Here the various departments of the Government are illustrated—the War, the Navy, the Patent, the Treasury, the Interior, the Post Office, and the Smithsonian Institution, &c. The Patent Office Department exhibits the original Declaration of Independence, and some relics of Washington. The Campbell Press, elsewhere on the grounds, prints facsimiles of the Declaration. Then there is the Women's Pavilion, covering an acre of ground, and costing $30,000, exhibiting the invention, skill, art and industry of the women of the world. Here is a $2,000 bonnet, made and presented by the ladies of New York. The principal of the other buildings are the Shoe and Leather, where one firm exhibits over 500 varieties of shoes, and another all the styles from 1776 down to this present time, and where all the shoe men lift up as their mottoes, "There is nothing like leather," "Keep pegging away," "Stick to your last." Various other industries are represented by separate buildings, either by the trade in general, or by individuals, as the Singer Sewing Machine, the Campbell Printing Press, &c., &c. Then there are the edifices erected by the various States and by Foreign Governments; some for the exhibition of goods, but mostly for the accommodation of its officers, and visiting citizens, and exhibitors. There are three English houses on the grounds especially worthy of observation. . . .

Statues and fountains adorn the grounds. There is the statue of Columbus, and one erected to Religious Liberty. There is a fountain erected by the Catholic Total Abstinence Union, costing $50,000, built of marble, with central rock work, surmounted

CENTENNIAL OF THE REPUBLIC 181

by a statue of Moses, and having four fountains jutting out, each surmounted with a statue of some prominent temperance man of the communion—Father Matthew, Charles Carroll, Archbishop Carroll, and Commodore Barry. Another fountain is that of Bartholdi, a French artist, in bronze, typifying light and water as twin goddesses of cities. This stands at the main entrance, between the main building and Machinery Hall. Immediately north of the latter building is a lake of five acres.

The West End Passenger Railway Company have three and a half miles of track on the grounds. Over this, giving a fair view of all the buildings, they run their cars at the rate of eight miles an hour, for five cents a trip each passenger. They have thirty-six cars, each holding eighty passengers. There are three or four stations. It affords a pleasing and cheap trip, and is a great convenience. Another convenience is the rolling chairs, manipulated by a company. There are one hundred of them. They may be hired, with a driver, for sixty cents per hour, or $4.50 a day, or without a driver for $1.00 for three hours. Another convenience, which people may carry with them, is a cane and chair combined. It costs $2.00, and weighs only twenty ounces. Catalogues of the contents of the several buildings are sold singly or combined on the grounds, and will often be found a great convenience.

There is a jury of awards, consisting of some 250 men, half of whom are foreigners. Their duty is to examine and compare articles exhibited, and give a diploma or medal and a written report to those who show the most meritoriously. For this service the foreign jurors are to receive $1,000 each, and the home jurors $600. A large and fine pavilion has been erected for their accommodation.

The articles on which the jury is to pass judgment have been arranged into twenty-eight groups: 1. Minerals, mining and metallurgy. 2. Pottery, glass, artificial stone, &c. 3. Chemistry and pharmacy, including the apparatus. 4. Animal and vegetable products, and the machinery for their preparation. 5. Fish and fish products, and apparatus of fishing, &c. 6. Timber, worked lumber, parts of buildings, forestry. 7. Furniture, upholstery, woodenware, baskets, &c. 8. Cotton, linen and other fabrics, including materials and machinery. 9. Wool and silk fabrics, including materials, and machinery. 10. Clothing, furs, India rubber goods, ornaments and fancy articles. 11. Jewelry, watches, silverware, bronzes, &c. 12. Leather and manufactures of leather. 13. Paper industry, stationery, printing and book making. 14. Apparatus of heating, lighting, ventilation, water supply and draining. 15. Builders' hardware, edge tools, cutlery, &c. 16. Military and sporting arms, weapons, apparatus of hunting, explosives, &c. 17. Carriages, vehicles and accessories. 18. Railway plans, rolling stock and apparatus, road engines, &c. 19. Vessels and apparatus of transportation. 20. Motors, hydraulic and pneumatic apparatus, &c.

CENTENNIAL OF THE REPUBLIC 183

21. Machine tools—wood, metal and stone. 22. Machines, apparatus and implements used in sewing and making clothing, lace, ornamental goods, pins, &c. 23. Agricultural, horticultural and gardening implements. 24. Instruments and apparatus of hygiene, surgery, medicine, prosthesis, &c. 25. Implements of precision, research, experiment and illustration, including topography and music. 26. Architecture and engineering. 27. Plastic and graphic art, sculpture. 28. Education and science. A simpler general division of objects to be illustrated by the Exposition was Agriculture, Art, Education, Horticulture, Machinery, Manufactures, Mining and Science—seven in all.

During the Exhibition there will be special days on the grounds, in the park and in the city, such as parades, society meetings, unveiling of statues, &c., regattas, the Fourth of July, &c.

Admission to the grounds has started at fifty cents, either in the form of one note or a silver half dollar. Nothing else is taken. A bank is on the grounds, and exchange offices at the several gates. There are thirteen general places of entrance, each of which has several sub-entrances, which can only be passed through in single file, a stile turning and registering, by electricity, the entrance. The grounds are open every day, except Sundays, from nine A. M. until six P. M. A change in all these points has been agitated, and will continue to be unless made. But this is the order, June 15th. Fifty cents gives admission to all the buildings, and all the sights and sounds. . . .

Around the grounds are numerous outside shows —as Operti's Garden, the Coliseum, Sawyer's Observatory, &c.

From the foundation of the world probably there has been no such exhibition, one on so extended a scale, and so full. And never, perhaps, has the rounding up of a century been celebrated so elaborately, and by so numerous a people, and through so great a length of time. The events which have called forth so grand a presentment are great, and worthy the study of mankind. The contrast which it creates between the Philadelphia of to-day and that of a hundred years ago is marvelous in its greatness and suddenness. The like will probably not be witnessed again by this generation.

THE HAYES-TILDEN PRESIDENTIAL CONTEST

By Edward Stanwood

THE election of Hayes, Ohio Republican, over Samuel J. Tilden, New York Democrat, in the Presidential campaign of 1876, was the most closely contested in the political history of the country. The electoral vote, as decided by a commission consisting of five Senators, five Representatives and five Supreme Court Justices, was 185 for Hayes and 184 for Tilden. This account of the long and bitter contest is from Stanwood's "History of Presidential Elections," published by Houghton Mifflin Company.

Hayes had a brilliant Civil War record, being brevetted major-general, but was unfortunate in running counter to the political leaders of his party during his Presidency. He stalwartly supported measures for the public welfare that were nullified by Congress, and opposed measures that were passed over his veto. His liberality in dealing with the South sowed the seeds of a prosperity such as it had not enjoyed since the War.

THE nomination of Rutherford B. Hayes was made unanimous on the seventh ballot. He was the only candidate who had made a gain on every vote; and as he was, if not very well known, entirely unobjectionable to the friends of all other candidates, it was less difficult to concentrate votes upon him than upon any other person in the list. Blaine, who was informed by telegraph at his house in Washington of the progress of the voting, wrote a dispatch congratulating Hayes immediately on receiving the result of the fifth vote.

The Democrats met at St. Louis two weeks later. The Convention was deprived of much of its interest by the fact that Tilden's lead for the nomination was so very great. He was known to have more than four hundred delegates out of the whole convention of 744, and while his candidacy was opposed, the opposition came from States which nevertheless chose unanimous delegations in his favor. The delegates chosen in the interest of other candidates were for the latter, but not against Tilden. His nomination was therefore universally expected, except by the more sanguine friends of other candidates. . . .

The polls had hardly closed on the day of election, the 7th of November, when the Democrats began to claim the Presidency. The returns came in so unfavorably for the Republicans that there was hardly a newspaper organ of the party which did not, on the following morning, concede the election of Tilden. He was believed to have carried every Southern State, as well as New York, Indiana, New Jersey and Connecticut. The whole number of electoral votes was 369. If the above estimate was correct, the Democratic candidates would have 203 votes, and the Republican candidates 166 votes. But word was sent out on the same day from Republican headquarters at Washington that Hayes and Wheeler were elected by one majority; that the States of South Carolina, Florida, and Louisiana had chosen Republican electors.

Then began the most extraordinary contest that ever took place in the country. The only hope of the Republicans was in the perfect defense of their position. The loss of a single vote would be fatal.

THE HAYES-TILDEN PRESIDENTIAL CONTEST 187

An adequate history of the four months between the popular election and the inauguration of Hayes would fill volumes. Space can be given here for only a bare reference to some of the most important events. Neither party was overscrupulous, and no doubt the acts of some members of each party were grossly illegal and corrupt. Certain transactions preceding the meetings of electors were not known until long afterward, when the key to the famous "cipher dispatches" was accidentally revealed.

In four States, South Carolina, Florida, Louisiana and Oregon, there were double returns. In South Carolina there were loud complaints that detachments of the army, stationed near the polls, had prevented a fair and free election. Although the Board of State Canvassers certified to the choice of the Hayes electors, who were chosen on the face of the returns, the Democratic candidates for electors met on the day fixed for the meeting of electors and cast ballots for Tilden and Hendricks. In Florida there were allegations of fraud on both sides. The canvassing board and the governor certified to the election of the Hayes electors, but, fortified by a court decision in their favor, the Democratic electors also met and voted. In Louisiana there was anarchy. There were two governors, two returning boards, two sets of returns showing different results, and two electoral colleges. In Oregon the Democratic governor adjudged one of the Republican electors ineligible, and gave a certificate to the highest candidate on the Democratic list.

The Republican electors, having no certificate from the governor, met and voted for Hayes and Wheeler. The Democratic elector, whose appointment was certified by the governor, appointed two others to fill the vacancies, when the two Republican electors would not meet with him, and the three voted for Tilden and Hendricks. All of these cases were very complicated in their incidents, and a brief account which should convey an intelligible idea of what occurred is impossible.

As soon as the electoral votes were cast it became a question of the very first importance how they were to be counted. It was evident that the Senate would refuse to be governed by the twenty-second joint rule —in fact, the Senate voted to rescind the rule—and it was further evident that if the count were to take place in accordance with that rule it would result in throwing out electoral votes on both sides on the most frivolous pretexts. It was asserted by the Republicans that, under the Constitution, the President of the Senate alone had the right to count, in spite of the fact that the joint rule, the work of their party, had assumed the power for the two Houses of Congress. On the other hand, the Democrats, who had always denounced that rule as unconstitutional, now maintained that the right to count was conferred upon Congress. A compromise became necessary, and the moderate men on both sides determined to effect the establishment of a tribunal, as evenly divided politically as might be, which should decide all disputed

THE HAYES-TILDEN PRESIDENTIAL CONTEST 189

questions so far as the Constitution gave authority to Congress to decide them. The outcome of their efforts was the Electoral Commission law of 1877, which was passed as originally reported. . . .

At the time the count began, on the 1st of February, 1877, each party was confident of victory. The Democrats relied upon a great variety of objections which had been prepared, the sustaining of any one of which would be sufficient to give the election to Tilden. The Republican hope was in a refusal of the commission to "go behind the returns." Senator Thomas W. Ferry, of Michigan, President "pro tempore" of the Senate, was the presiding officer. The count proceeded, under the law, in the alphabetical order of the States. When the vote of Florida was reached, the certificates of the Hayes and also of the Tilden electors were read. Objections were made to each. The Democrats asserted that the Hayes electors were not duly chosen; that the certificate of the governor to their election was the result of a conspiracy; that its validity, if any, had been annulled by a subsequent certificate by the governor, to the effect that the Tilden electors were chosen; that a court decision made certain the election of the Democratic electors; and that one of the Republican electors was a shipping commissioner under appointment from the Government of the United States at the time of his election, and was therefore disqualified. The Republican objection to the Tilden votes was that the returns were not only authenticated by any person holding at the time an office under the State of Florida. It was only on the 7th of February that the commission, after very long arguments by eminent counsel selected to appear for the two parties, decided the case of Florida.

The decision was that it was not competent for the commission "to go into evidence 'aliunde' the papers opened by the President of the Senate, to prove that other persons than those regularly certified to by the governor" were appointed. With reference to the case of the elector alleged to have been disqualified, it was decided that the evidence did not show that he held office on the day of his appointment. The several votes were passed by eight to seven—all the Republicans being on one side, and all the Democrats on the other. The formal decision, which was submitted to the two Houses, was that the four Hayes electors, naming them, were duly appointed electors, and that their votes were the constitutional votes. The Houses met on February 10, and received this decision. Formal objection was then made to the decision of the Electoral Commission, and the Houses separated to consider it. The Senate, by a strict party vote, decided that the votes should be counted. The House of Representatives, by a vote which was on party lines, except that one Democrat voted with the Republicans, voted that the electoral votes given by the Tilden electors should be counted. The two Houses not having agreed in rejecting the decision of the commission, it stood, and the joint session was resumed. The votes of Florida having been recorded, the count proceeded until Louisiana was reached.

The Republican objections to the Tilden votes from Louisiana were, like those to the votes of Florida, brief and formal. The government, of which W. P. Kellogg was the head, had been recognized by every department of the Government of the United States as the true government of Louisiana, and the certificates of the Hayes electors certified by him were in due form. The Democrats made a great variety of objections to the Hayes votes. They asserted that John McEnery was the lawful Governor of the State; that the certificates asserting the appointment of the Hayes electors were false; and that the canvass of votes by the returning board was without jurisdiction and void. Special objection was made to three of the electors; to two of them as being disqualified, under the Constitution; and to the third, Governor Kellogg, because he certified to his own election. Several days were consumed in argument before the commission. On the 16th of February the commission voted, once more by eight to seven, that the evidence offered to prove that the Tilden electors were chosen be not received, and that the certificates of the Hayes electors were the true votes of Louisiana. The decision having been communicated to the two Houses, the count was resumed on the 19th. Objection was made to the decision of the commission, and the two Houses separated again to act upon them. The Senate voted, by 41 to 28, that the decision of the commission should stand. The House voted that the electoral votes cast by the Hayes electors for Louisiana ought not to be counted—173 to 99. In each case this was a party vote, except that two Republicans in the House voted with the Democrats. . . .

To the Hayes votes in South Carolina the Democrats next objected that there was no legal election in the State, that there was not, in South Carolina, during the year 1876, a Republican form of government, and that the army and the United States deputy marshals stationed at and near the polls prevented the free exercise of the right of suffrage. The Republicans asserted that the Tilden board was not duly appointed, and that the certificates were wholly defective in form and lacking the necessary official certification. The papers having been referred to the Electoral Commission, that body met again on the 26th. Senator Thurman was obliged to retire from service upon the commission, on account of illness, and Senator Francis Kernan was substituted for him. After a day devoted to arguments, the commission voted unanimously that the Tilden electors were not the true electors of South Carolina, and, by the old majority of eight to seven, that the Hayes electors were the constitutional electors duly appointed. The two Houses separated upon renewed objections to the decision of the commission, and as before the Senate sustained the finding, while the House voted to reject it. . . .

Question after question was decided uniformly in favor of the Republicans. It became evident to the Democrats that their case was lost. They charged gross partisanship upon the Republican members of the Electoral Commission, in determining every point involved in the dual returns for their own party, though as a matter of fact there does not seem to have been much room for choice between the two parties on the score of partisanship. Each member of the commission favored by his vote that view which would result in adding to the electoral vote of his own party. But as the result of the count became more and more certainly a Republican triumph, the anger of the Democrats rose. Some of them were for discontinuing the count; and the symptoms of a disposition to filibuster so that there should be no declaration of the result gave reason for public disquietude. But the conservative members of the party were too patriotic to allow the failure of a law which they had been instrumental in passing to lead to anarchy or revolution, and they sternly discountenanced all attempts to defeat the conclusion of the count. The summing up of the votes was read by Mr. Allison on the 2d of March, amid great excitement. . . .

Mr. Ferry thereupon declared Rutherford B. Hayes elected President, and William A. Wheeler Vice-President, of the United States. The decision was acquiesced in peaceably by the whole country, and by men of every party. But the Democrats have never ceased to denounce the whole affair as a fraud, and some newspapers have steadily refused to speak of Hayes as having ever been rightfully in possession of the Presidential office. Their anger at the time was very great, since they believed that Tilden was fairly elected.

CUSTER'S LAST STAND

By Judson Elliott Walker

THAT Lieutenant-Colonel George A. Custer, who had been brevetted major-general for distinguished services in Grant's last campaign of the Civil War, should have gone to his death in 1876 bearing President Grant's animosity, is a regretful matter of record. In his "Campaign of General Custer in the North-West," from which this account is taken, Walker, the historian, relates that Custer was to have commanded one of the three army divisions operating against the Indians under Sitting Bull and Crazy Horse in the Black Hills country. Unfortunately he was called to Washington, and angered Grant by giving distasteful testimony before the Congressional Committee engaged in investigating charges against Secretary Belknap, reflecting upon Grant's brother, Orville, a frontier post-trader. Displaced as head of the division, Custer secured a modification of the Presidential order, and on June 25, 1876, led his Seventh Cavalry to death by massacre, not a man surviving.

IN the spring of 1876 it was determined by the Government to attempt the subjugation of Sitting Bull and the lawless tribes under him, who had refused to accede to the provisions of the treaty of 1868, and had since led a wandering life. Their numbers augmented each spring by frequent accessions of warriors, and supplies of war from the Missouri River Agencies. From their stronghold at the headwaters of the Yellowstone, war parties were continually sent out to annoy the white settlements.

Their camp formed a convenient retreat for disaffected Agency Indians. Criminals and unruly spirits, supported by the Government through the winter, were ready in the summer to join the hostiles, conveying to them arms, ammunition, ponies and supplies. Thus the problem of dealing with the professedly peaceful Indians was greatly complicated.

The only way to end the constantly-recurring troubles, and prevent a general uprising of the whole body of Indians—many of them already on the warpath, resentful at the violation of the treaty of 1868—was to strike a decisive blow directly at the headquarters of the savage tribes, and by breaking up their rendezvous in the Yellowstone region, compel them to return and surrender at the various Agencies on the Missouri River.

With this object in view, the expedition of 1876 was planned. It was arranged that three expeditions should start simultaneously for the headwaters of the Yellowstone—one from the north, one from the south, and one from the east—the three to join forces and coöperate in the region constituting the objective point of their converging marches.

The column from the south, under General Crook, started from Fort Fetterman, Wyoming Territory, May 29th, 1876, and marched due north for the Powder River country. It was composed of 1,300 men, and arrived at old Fort Reno June 3d. It succeeded in reaching the indicated ground, viz., the valley of the Yellowstone, drained by its tributaries, the Big Horn, Rosebud, Tongue and Powder Rivers, together with their branches, and at one time was within one hundred miles of the northern column; but the

Indians were between them, and after several heavy skirmishes, in which the troops were defeated, it fell back to the head of Tongue River, and from there returned ingloriously to its starting place.

The force from the north, under Colonel Gibbon, left Fort Ellis, Montana, with a strength of four hundred men, and wagon train, marched due east, and joined the force from the east under General Terry, June 1st.

The departure of the column from the east, which, in the original plan of the campaign, was to have been led by Lieutenant-Colonel Custer, had been delayed, in consequence of Custer having been called to Washington to give evidence before the Congressional Committee then engaged in investigating charges against Secretary of War Belknap. Like all army officers stationed on the frontier, Custer was conversant with the terrible corruption of the Interior Department, displayed in the management of the Indian Agencies and trading posts. As an honest man, he did what many others, better informed than himself, but more devoted to self-interest, had not dared to do—spoke aloud his convictions. Custer's testimony—and the fact that he had presumed to hold opinions on the subject—was distasteful to Belknap's friend, U. S. Grant, President of the United States, and brother of Orville Grant, a post-trader of precious memory on the Missouri River. . . .

Custer was displaced from the command of the eastern column, then in process of organization, at Fort

Lincoln, and forbidden, by order of the President, to accompany the troops on the march. General Terry was placed in command of the expedition, but afterward, in response to the earnest entreaties of Custer to be spared the humiliation of seeing the troops march without him, the President's order was so far modified as to permit him to go with the expedition, in command of the 7th Cavalry. Thus reorganized, the column left Fort Lincoln with 12 companies of the 7th Cavalry, under Lieutenant-Colonel Custer, 3 companies of the 6th and 17th Infantry, 4 Gatling guns, and a detachment of 45 Indian scouts, under the Arickiree chief, Bloody Knife. . . . These three columns started from the circumference of a circle with a radius of three hundred miles, under orders to concentrate and join their converging lines somewhere in the region enclosed by the Big Horn and Powder Rivers—where the enemy was supposed to be in force—there to enclose and crush out the desperate remnants of savage outlaws, their number being variously estimated at from 1,000 to 3,000. Later events proved the fallacy of this belief; that between 3,000 and 5,000 Indians were massed in the fatal valley of the Yellowstone, awaiting in savage ferocity the coming of the troops, all of whom they could easily have annihilated with their superior arms and steeds, had the remainder of them come within their lines.

Who that lived in Bismarck in the year 1876, during the time that the "Lincoln column" of the great expedition was being fitted out across the river, will forget that it was matter of public notoriety that the savage hordes were gathering their clans from north and from south, to dispute the passage of the soldiers; that even while their godly agents were crying aloud, "All is well," the Red Cloud, Standing Rock and Spotted Tail agencies were being depopulated of their fighting material. Supply trains, with men, arms, ponies, provisions, ammunition and warriors, were rushing to that wild rendezvous on the Yellowstone, where the restless Sitting Bull awaited the tardy coming of the royal sacrifice. Each new accession to their ranks was hailed with acclamations of delight and in the weird gyrations of the war-dance the blood-stained wretches recounted their gory deeds, and sought to stimulate each other to horrid acts of brutality and bloodshed. Who that heard them can forget those significant inquiries heard in the streets of Bismarck, by emissaries fresh from Sitting Bull's camp, during the sad days of Custer's humiliation under Presidential displeasure, when the men waited in arms for the order to march, and their brave, outspoken commander chafed in bitterness of spirit under the undeserved disgrace of being ordered to stay behind. "What are the dog-soldiers waiting for?" "Are they tired before they start?" "What is the matter with Custer?" "Is the long-haired chief sick?" All these and more, coupled with direful threats and sickening messages of expectant revenge, from Rain-in-the-Face and his no less bloody followers, were repeated from mouth to mouth, and excited in many hearts sad feelings of foreboding relative to the fate of the gallant Custer, who in going forth to give battle to the merciless chieftain of the Sioux, left behind him, in the person of U. S. Grant, the chief executive of the land, a foe no less relentless. . . .

. . . Lieutenant-Colonel Custer was not hampered by positive orders, being simply advised to follow the Indian trail until its general direction was definitely ascertained. Then, if, as was expected, it should be found to turn toward the Little Big Horn, he was directed to proceed southward as far as the headwaters of the Tongue, and then to turn toward the Little Big Horn, guarding constantly against the possibility of the Indians escaping around his left flank to the south and rear, General Terry distinctly stating that "such was his confidence in the zeal, energy and ability of Lieutenant-Colonel Custer, that he would not impose upon him precise orders, which might hamper his action when nearly in contact with the enemy."

Thus, with his future course of action left to his own discretionary judgment, Lieutenant-Colonel Custer, with his regiment, left camp on the Yellowstone, June 22d, and proceeded up the Rosebud River during the 23d and 24th, making sixty-one miles, the trail and Indian signs freshening with every mile, when they encamped and waited for information from the scouts, whose detachment had accompanied the regiment. It was ascertained, beyond doubt, that the

Indian village was in the valley of the Little Big Horn, and, in order to reach it without discovering their approach to the Indians, a night march was decided on, the troops moving at 11 P. M., the line of march turning from the Rosebud to the right, up one of its branches. At 2 P. M. of the morning of the 25th, it was ascertained that the divide between the Rosebud and the Little Big Horn Rivers could not be crossed before daylight. The command then rested for three hours and made coffee, many of the brave fellows then partaking of their last meal on earth. The march was then resumed and the divide crossed, and about 8 A. M. the command was in the valley of one of the branches of the Little Big Horn. Indians being then plainly seen, and as it was thus evident that the troops could not take them by surprise, it was decided to attack them at once.

On the march, Custer had divided the regiment into three separate commands, assigning to Major M. A. Reno, Companies M, A and G, and to Captain Benteen, H, D and K, retaining himself the command of Companies C, E, F, I and L; Captain McDougal being assigned with Company B to the care of the pack train in the rear.

Custer's plan of attack in Indian warfare, in which he had been hitherto preëminently successful, was that of simultaneous assault from several points, an attack in front and flank at all events. In this instance, when arrived near the battlefield, and as he prepared himself to lead the charge, about 12.30 P. M., he ordered the remaining two divisions to move up quickly and support him.

The battalion under Benteen with the pack train did not come up in time to participate in the charge and opening fight.

The detachment under Major Reno, numbering 145 men, hurried forward as ordered, and crossed the river, where they soon became engaged with overwhelming numbers of the enemy. To save themselves from utter annihilation at the hands of the countless droves of Indians, who suddenly sprang into view, they retreated to a high hill in the vicinity, where they entrenched themselves, being soon after joined by the troops under Benteen.

Soon afterward they were furiously attacked and besieged by numberless foes; the siege being next day renewed, when the troops were relieved by the arrival of the soldiers under General Terry, the Indians filing away across the hills at his approach.

Up to this date nothing was known of the fate of Custer and his command, the soldiers in the entrenchment on the hill, who never before had known him to fail them in danger, wondering audibly why he did not come to their relief. . . .

Upon the arrival of General Terry, the first intimation was obtained of the fate of Custer and his men. An Upsaroka scout, named Curley, had almost miraculously escaped during the progress of the fight with Custer, and made his way back to General Terry, then on the steamer "Far West," at the mouth of the Big Horn River, and reported the total loss of Custer and his soldiers.

This report was disbelieved, or, at least, thought to be greatly exaggerated—it being deemed impossible that such a calamity could befall the most successful Indian fighter of his day. Yet, from the extreme agitation of the forlorn scout, it was evident that a misfortune of some kind had occurred; and General Terry, with the residue of the troops under him, at once pressed forward, under the leadership of Curley, arriving in time to save the lives of the wearied survivors under Reno; who, though making a gallant defense against overpowering numbers of the enemy, had lost all hope of rescue, since Custer had apparently failed them, and greeted the unexpected arrival of their comrades as a happy reprieve from expected death.

Immediately upon the arrival of General Terry—the Indians then having left—a detachment was sent out to search for traces of the missing commander and his men. Not far away their battlefield was found, and though no living thing was there to tell how grandly they had fought, and nobly they had died, yet no tongue was needed to show that they had all gone down, company by company, contending to the last for life, as heroes ever do. Their dead and mutilated bodies, disposed in the orderly array of systematic battle; the compact companies, with officers in place behind them; the unbroken skirmish line of ghastly corpses, testified more eloquently than spoken words could do to the sublimity of courage that had animated each soul of that heroic band. An examination of the battleground disclosed the fact that when Custer left his comrades of the other two divisions, with orders for them to hasten forward and join in the attack, he dashed down the stream some distance, seeking a convenient ford where he could cross the river and attack the village from below; but failing to do so, went much further down the river than intended in his arrangements with Reno, whom he expected to support in the charge he had ordered Reno to make before leaving him. When, at length, a suitable ford was discovered, his further progress was violently opposed by numberless Indians, who poured in a heavy fire from across the narrow river. Custer dismounted, to fight on foot, but his skirmishers were unable to cross the stream under the galling fire that assailed them and the cavalry were speedily driven back to the high ground in the rear; but not until swarms of Indians, mounted and on foot, had poured over the shallow river, and seized the ravines on either side, effectually cutting off their retreat in the direction in which they came. Custer was soon effectually surrounded, and receiving a terrible fire from all sides. The dead bodies of men and horses were found at the ford, and at a distance of about three-quarters of a mile from the river, as though thrown across the line of retreat to check the advance of the enemy. The entire company of Captain James Calhoun, brother-in-law of Lieutenant-

Colonel Custer, lay dead in an irregular line, with Captain Calhoun and his Lieutenant, John J. Crittenden, in their proper places in the rear. A mile beyond this, on a ridge parallel to the river, the whole of Captain Myles W. Keogh's company were slaughtered in position—their right resting on the hill where Custer fell. Still further back on the ridge were found the dead bodies of thirty-two men of Captain George W. Yates' company, and here, too, had fallen the brave and ill-fated Custer, with his brother, Captain T. W. Custer, his Adjutant, Captain W. W. Cook, Lieutenant William Van W. Reily, and Captain Yates, together with the young nephew and brother of Custer—Armstrong Reed and Boston Custer, forage-master of the 7th Cavalry.

In a ravine near the river were found the dead bodies of the men and horses of Captain Thomas W. Custer's company, together with those of Captain Algernon E. Smith, and twenty-three men of his company. . . .

The probable fate of thirty-five missing men and their three officers is too horrible to contemplate without a shudder. It is claimed by Indians who were in the fight and afterwards returned to their agencies, that the horses of a portion of the cavalry were captured by the Indians early in the engagement, while the situation of those surrounding the group of men and officers, with whom Custer made his last stand, would seem to indicate that they had been killed by the soldiers to form a barricade, behind which to defend themselves, until the relief which they doubtless then expected from Reno and Benteen should arrive.

THE COMING OF THE TELEPHONE

By Thomas A. Watson

WATSON was an expert machinist and pioneer electrician who greatly assisted Alexander Graham Bell in the discovery and early construction of the telephone. This address, delivered at Chicago in 1913, before the Third Annual Convention of the Telephone Pioneers of America, is reprinted from The Telephone Review. *It recounts the memorable June 2, 1875, when a sound was first electrically transmitted and "the speaking telephone was born," at 109 Court Street, Boston. Directed by Bell, Watson "made the first telephone, put up the first telephone wire and heard the first words ever uttered through a telephone." They were, "Mr. Watson, please come here, I want you."*

On February 14, 1876, Bell received a patent for his speaking telephone. Though his claims were disputed by other inventors, his rights were sustained by the United States Supreme Court, and he is given credit for being the first to perfect and construct a working instrument.

I AM to speak to you of the birth and babyhood of the telephone, and something of the events which preceded that important occasion. These are matters that must seem to you ancient history; in fact, they seem so to me, although the events all happened less than 40 years ago, in the years 1874 to 1880. . . .

I realize now what a lucky boy I was, when at 13 years of age I had to leave school and go to work for my living, although I didn't think so at that time. . . . There's a "tide in the affairs of men," you know, and that was the beginning of its flood in my life, for after trying several vocations—clerking, bookkeeping, carpentering, etc.

—and finding them all unattractive, I at last found just the job that suited me in the electrical workshop of Charles Williams, at 109 Court Street, Boston—one of the best men I have ever known. Better luck couldn't befall a boy than to be brought so early in life under the influence of such a high-minded gentleman as Charles Williams. . . .

Besides the regular work at Williams', there was a constant stream of wild-eyed inventors, with big ideas in their heads and little money in their pockets, coming to the shop to have their ideas tried out in brass and iron. . . .

. . . Among them was dear old Moses G. Farmer, perhaps the leading practical electrician of that day. He was full of good ideas, which he was constantly bringing to Williams to have worked out. I did much of his work and learned from him more about electricity than ever before or since. He was electrician at that time for the United States Torpedo Station at Newport, Rhode Island, and in the early winter of 1874, I was making for him some experimental torpedo exploding apparatus. That apparatus will always be connected in my mind with the telephone, for one day when I was hard at work on it, a tall, slender, quick-motioned man with pale face, black side-whiskers, and drooping mustache, big nose and high sloping forehead crowned with bushy, jet black hair, came rushing out of the office and over to my work bench. It was Alexander Graham Bell, whom I saw then for the first time. He was bringing to me a piece of mechanism which I had made for him under instructions from the office. It had not been made as he had directed and he had broken down the rudimentary discipline of the shop in coming directly to me to get it altered. It was a receiver and a transmitter of his "Harmonic Telegraph," an invention of his with which he was then endeavoring to win fame and fortune. It was a simple affair by means of which, utilizing the law of sympathetic vibration, he expected to send six or eight Morse messages on a single wire at the same time, without interference.

Although most of you are probably familiar with the device, I must, to make my story clear, give you a brief description of the instruments, for though Bell never succeeded in perfecting his telegraph, his experimenting on it led to a discovery of the highest importance.

The essential parts of both transmitter and receiver were an electro-magnet and a flattened piece of steel clock spring. The spring was clamped by one end to one pole of the magnet, and had its other end free to vibrate over the other pole. The transmitter had, besides this, make-and-break points like an ordinary vibrating bell which, when the current was on, kept the spring vibrating in a sort of nasal whine, of a pitch corresponding to the pitch of the spring. When the signaling key was closed, an electrical copy of that whine passed through the wire and the distant receiver. There were, say, six transmitters with their springs tuned to six different pitches and six receivers with their springs tuned to correspond. Now, theoretically, when a transmitter sent its electrical whine into the line wire, its own faithful receiver spring at the distant station would wriggle sympathetically but all the others on the same line would remain coldly quiescent. Even when all the transmitters were whining at once through their entire gamut, making a row as if all the miseries this world of trouble ever produced were concentrated there, each receiver spring along the line would select its own from that sea of troubles and ignore all the others. Just see what a simple, sure-to-work invention this was; for just break up those various whines into the dots and dashes of Morse messages and one wire would do the work of six, and the "Duplex" telegraph that had just been invented would be beaten to a frazzle. Bell's reward would be immediate and rich, for the "Duplex" had been bought by the Atlantic and Pacific Telegraph Company, giving them a great advantage over their only competitor, the Western Union Company, and the latter would, of course, buy Bell's invention and his financial problems would be solved.

All this was, as I have said, theoretical, and it was mighty lucky for Graham Bell that it was, for had his harmonic telegraph been a well behaved apparatus that always did what its parent wanted it to do, the speaking telephone might never have emerged from a certain marvelous conception, that had even then been surging back of Bell's high forehead for two or three years. What that conception was, I soon learned, for he couldn't help speaking about it, although his friends tried to hush it up. They didn't like to have him get the reputation of being visionary, or—something worse.

To go on with my story; after Mr. Farmer's peacemaking machines were finished, I made half a dozen pairs of the harmonic instruments for Bell. He was surprised, when he tried them to find that they didn't work as well as he expected. The cynical Watson wasn't at all surprised, for he had never seen anything electrical yet that worked at first the way the inventor thought it would. Bell wasn't discouraged in the least and a long course of experiments followed which gave me a steady job that winter and brought me into close contact with a wonderful personality that did more to mold my life rightly than anything else that ever came into it.

I became mightily tired of those "whiners" that winter. I call them by that name, perhaps, as an inadequate expression of my disgust with their persistent perversity, the struggle with which soon began to take all the joy out of my young life, not being endowed with the power of Macbeth's weird sisters to

"Look into the seeds of time,
And say which grain will grow and which will not."

Let me say here, that I have always had a feeling of respect for Elisha Gray, who, a few years later, made that harmonic telegraph work, and vibrate well-behaved messages, that would go where they were sent, without fooling with every receiver on the line. . . .

Mr. Bell was very apt to do his experimenting at night, for he was busy during the day at the Boston University, where he was Professor of Vocal Physiology, especially teaching his father's system of visible speech, by which a deaf mute might learn to talk—quite significant of what Bell was soon to do in making mute metal talk. For this reason I would often remain at the shop during the evening to help him test some improvement he had had me make on the instruments.

One evening when we were resting from our struggles with the apparatus, Bell said to me: "Watson, I want to tell you of another idea I have, which I think will surprise you." I listened, I suspect, somewhat languidly, for I must have been working that day about sixteen hours, with only a short nutritive interval, and Bell had already given me, during the weeks we had worked together, more new ideas on a great variety of subjects, including visible speech, elocution and flying machines, than my brain could assimilate, but when he went on to say that he had an idea by which he believed it would be possible to talk by telegraph, my nervous system got such a shock that the tired feeling vanished. I have never forgotten his exact words; they have run in my mind ever since like a mathematical formula. "If," he said, "I could make a current of electricity vary in intensity, precisely as the air varies in density during the production of a sound, I should be able to transmit speech telegraphically." He then sketched for me an instrument that he thought would do this, and we discussed the possibility of constructing one. I did not make it; it was altogether too costly, and the chances of its working too uncertain to impress his financial backers —Mr. Gardiner G. Hubbard and Mr. Thomas Sanders —who were insisting that the wisest thing for Bell to do was to perfect the harmonic telegraph; then he would have money and leisure enough to build air castles like the telephone. . . .

If the exact time could be fixed, the date when the conception of the undulatory or speech-transmitting current took its perfect form in Bell's mind would be the greatest day in the history of the telephone, but certainly June 2, 1875, must always rank next; for on that day the mocking fiend inhabiting that demonic telegraph apparatus, just as a now-you-see-it-and-now-you-don't sort of a satanic joke, opened the curtain that hides from man great Nature's secrets and gave us a glimpse as quick as if it were through the shutter of a snap-shot camera, into that treasury of things not yet discovered. That imp didn't do this in any kindly, helpful spirit—any inventor knows he isn't that kind of a being—he just meant to tantalize and prove that a man is too stupid to grasp a secret, even if it is revealed to him. But he hadn't properly estimated Bell, though he had probably sized me up all right. That glimpse was enough to let Bell see and seize the very thing he had been dreaming about and drag it out into the world of human affairs.

Coming back to earth, I'll try and tell you what happened that day. In the experiments on the harmonic telegraph, Bell had found that the reason why the messages got mixed up was inaccuracy in the adjustment of the pitches of the receiver springs to those of the transmitter. Bell always had to do this tuning himself, as my sense of pitch and knowledge of music were quite lacking—a faculty (or lackulty) which you will hear later became quite useful. Mr. Bell was in the habit of observing the pitch of a spring by pressing it against his ear while the corresponding transmitter in a distant room was sending its intermittent current through the magnet of that receiver. He would then manipulate the tuning screw until that spring was tuned to accord with the pitch of the whine coming from the transmitter. All this experimenting was carried on in the upper story of the Williams building, where we had a wire connecting two rooms perhaps sixty feet apart looking out on Court Street.

On the afternoon of June 2, 1875, we were hard at work on the same old job, testing some modification of the instruments. Things were badly out of tune that afternoon in that hot garret, not only the instruments, but, I fancy, my enthusiasm and my temper, though Bell was as energetic as ever. I had charge of the transmitters as usual, setting them squealing one after the other, while Bell was retuning the receiver springs one by one, pressing them against his ear as I have described. One of the transmitter springs I was attending to stopped vibrating and I plucked it to start it again. It didn't start and I kept on plucking it, when suddenly I heard a shout from Bell in the next room, and then out he came with a rush, demanding, "What did you do then? Don't change anything. Let me see!" I showed him. It was very simple. The make-and-break points of the transmitter spring I was trying to start had become welded together, so that when I snapped the spring the circuit had remained unbroken while that strip of magnetized steel by its vibration over the pole of its magnet, was generating that marvelous conception of Bell's—a current of electricity that varied in intensity precisely as the air was varying in density within hearing distance of that spring. That undulatory current had passed through the connecting wire to the distant receiver which, fortunately, was a mechanism that could transform that current back into an extremely faint echo of the sound of the vibrating spring that had generated it, but what was still more fortunate, the right man had that mechanism at his ear during that fleeting moment, and instantly recognized the transcendent importance of that faint sound thus electrically transmitted. The shout I heard and his excited rush into my room were the result of that recognition. The speaking telephone was born at that moment. Bell knew perfectly well that the mechanism that could transmit all the complex vibrations of one sound could do the same for any sound, even that of speech. That experiment showed him that the complex apparatus he had thought would be needed to accomplish that long dreamed result was not at all necessary, for here was an extremely simple mechanism operating in a perfectly obvious way, that could do it perfectly. All the experimenting that followed that discovery, up to the time the telephone was put into practical use was largely a matter of working out the details. We spent a few hours verifying the discovery, repeating it with all the differently tuned springs we had, and before we parted that night Bell gave me directions for making the first electric speaking telephone. I was to mount a small drumhead of gold beater's skin over one of the receivers, join the center of the drumhead to the free end of the receiver spring and arrange a mouthpiece over the drumhead to talk into. His idea was to force the steel spring to follow the vocal vibrations and generate a current of electricity that would vary in intensity as the air varies in density during the utterance of speech sounds. I followed these directions and had the instrument ready for its trial the very next day. I rushed it, for Bell's excitement and enthusiasm over the discovery had aroused mine again, which had been sadly dampened during those last few weeks by the meager results of the harmonic experiments. I made every part of that first telephone myself, but I didn't realize while I was working on it what a tremendously important piece of work I was doing.

The two rooms in the attic were too near together for the test, as our voices would be heard through the air, so I ran a wire especially for the trial from one of the rooms in the attic down two flights to the third floor where Williams' main shop was, ending it near my work bench at the back of the building. That was the first telephone line. You can well imagine that both our hearts were beating above the normal rate, while we were getting ready for the trial of the new instrument that evening. I got more satisfaction from the experiment than Mr. Bell did, for shout my best I could not make him hear me, but I could hear his voice and almost catch the words. I rushed upstairs and told him what I had heard. It was enough to show him that he was on the right track, and before he left that night he gave me directions for several improvements in the telephones I was to have ready for the next trial.

I hope my pride in the fact that I made the first telephone, put up the first telephone wire and heard the first words ever uttered through a telephone, has never been too ostentatious and offensive to my friends, but I am sure that you will grant that a reasonable amount of that human weakness is excusable in me. My pride has been tempered to quite a bearable degree by my realization that the reason why I heard Bell in that first trial of the telephone and he did not hear me, was the vast superiority of his strong vibratory tones over any sound my undeveloped voice was then able to utter. My sense of hearing, however, has always been unusually acute, and that might have helped to determine this result.

The building where these first telephone experiments were made is still in existence. It is now used as a theater. The lower stories have been much altered, but that attic is still quite unchanged and a few weeks ago I stood on the very spot where I snapped those springs and helped test the first telephone thirty-seven years and seven months before.

Of course, in our struggle to expel the imps from the invention, an immense amount of experimenting had to be done, but it wasn't many days before we could talk back and forth and hear each other's voice. It is, however, hard for me to realize now that it was not until the following March that I heard a complete and intelligible sentence. It made such an impression upon me that I wrote that first sentence in a book I have always preserved. The occasion had not been arranged and rehearsed as I suspect the sending of the first message over the Morse telegraph had been years before, for instead of that noble first telegraphic message—"What hath God wrought?" the first message of the telephone was: "Mr. Watson, please come here, I want you." Perhaps, if Mr. Bell had realized that he was about to make a bit of history, he would have been prepared with a more sounding and interesting sentence.

Soon after the first telephones were made, Bell hired two rooms on the top floor of an inexpensive boarding house at No. 5 Exeter Place, Boston, since demolished to make room for mercantile buildings. He slept in one room; the other he fitted up as a laboratory. I ran a wire for him between the two rooms and after that time practically all his experimenting was done there. It was here one evening when I had gone there to help him test some improvement and to spend the night with him, that I heard the first complete sentence I have just told you about. Matters began to move more rapidly and during the summer of 1876, the telephone was talking so well that one didn't have to ask the other man to say it over again more than three or four times before one could understand quite well, if the sentences were simple.

This was the year of the Centennial Exposition at Philadelphia, and Bell decided to make an exhibit there. I was still working for Williams, and one of the jobs I did for Bell was to construct a telephone of each form that had been devised up to that time. These were the first nicely finished instruments that had been made. There had been no money nor time to waste on polish or non-essentials. But these Centennial telephones were done up in the highest style of the art. You could see your face in them. These aristocratic telephones worked finely, in spite of their glitter, when Sir William Thompson tried them at Philadelphia that summer. I was proud as Bell himself, when I read Sir William's report, wherein he said after giving an account of the tests: "I need hardly say I was astonished and delighted, so were the others who witnessed the experiment and verified with their own ears the electric transmission of speech. This, perhaps, the greatest marvel hitherto achieved by electric telegraph, has been obtained by appliances of quite a homespun and rudimentary character." I have never forgiven Sir William for that last line. Homespun!

UNCLE SAM RESUMES SPECIE PAYMENTS

By Secretary of the Treasury John Sherman

GOVERNMENT specie payments had been suspended since 1861, and a law providing for their resumption was passed by Congress in 1875. It was to take effect January 1, 1879. During the interval it was the object of repeated attack, but all efforts to repeal it failed.

The Resumption Act authorized the Secretary of the Treasury to amass an adequate supply of gold wherewith to resume specie payments. John Sherman was Secretary when the act became operative. This article is from his "Recollections of Forty Years in the House, Senate and Cabinet" (Superior Printing Company). By the sale of bonds at favorable opportunities, Sherman had on hand $140,000,000 in gold on the resumption date, which passed off without the dreaded shock materializing. Sherman was a younger brother of the General who led the famous "march to the sea."

ON the 1st of January, 1879, when the resumption act went into effect, the aggregate amount of gold coin and bullion in the Treasury exceeded $140,000,000. United States notes, when presented, were redeemed with gold coin, but instead of the notes being presented for redemption, gold coin in exchange for them was deposited, thus increasing the gold in the Treasury.

The resumption of specie payments was generally accepted as a fortunate event by the great body of the people of the United States, but there was a great diversity of opinion as to what was meant by resumption. The commercial and banking classes generally treated resumption as if it involved the payment and cancellation of United States notes and all forms of government money except coin and bank notes. Another class was opposed to resumption, and favored a large issue of paper money without any promise or expectation of redemption in coin. The body of the people, I believe, agreed with me in opinion that resumption meant, not the cancellation and withdrawal of greenbacks, but the bringing them up to par and maintaining them as the equivalent of coin by the payment of them in coin on demand by the holder. This was my definition of resumption. I do not believe that any commercial nation can conduct modern operations of business upon the basis of coin alone. Prior to our Civil War the United States undertook to collect its taxes in specie and to pay specie for its obligations; this was the bullion theory. This narrow view of money compelled the States to supply paper currency, and this led to a great diversity of money, depending upon the credit, the habits and the wants of the people of the different States. The United States notes, commonly called greenbacks, were the creature of necessity, but proved a great blessing, and only needed one attribute to make them the best substitute for coin money that has ever been devised. That quality was supplied by their redemption in coin, when demanded by the holder.

The feeling in the Treasury Department on the day of resumption is thus described by J. K. Upton, Assistant Secretary, in an article written at the close of 1892:

"The year, however, closed with no unpleasant excitement, but with unpleasant forebodings. The 1st day of January was Sunday and no business was transacted. On Monday anxiety reigned in the office of the Secretary. Hour after hour passed; no news came from New York. Inquiry by wire showed all was quiet. At the close of business came this message: '$135,000 of notes presented for coin—$400,000 of gold for notes.' That was all. Resumption was accomplished with no disturbance. By five o'clock the news was all over the land, and the New York bankers were sipping their tea in absolute safety.

"Thirteen years have since passed, and the redemption fund still remains intact in the sub-treasury vaults. The prediction of the Secretary has become history. When gold could with certainty be obtained for notes, nobody wanted it. The experiment of maintaining a limited amount of United States notes in circulation, based upon a reasonable reserve in the Treasury pledged for that purpose, and supported also by the credit of the government, has proved generally satisfactory, and the exclusive use of these notes for circulation may become, in time, the fixed financial policy of the government."

The immediate effect of resumption of specie payments was to advance the public credit, which made it possible to rapidly fund all the bonds of the United States then redeemable into bonds bearing four per cent. interest. . . .

... Letters written about this date will show my view better than anything I can say now. ...

Washington, D. C., January 8, 1879.
R. C. Stone, Esq., Secretary Bullion Club, New York. ...

I regret that my official duties will not permit me, in person, to respond to the toast you send me, and I cannot do so, by letter, in words more expressive than the toast itself, "To Resumption—may it be forever."

Irredeemable money is always the result of war, pestilence, or some great misfortune. A nation would not, except in dire necessity, issue its promises to pay money when it is unable to redeem those promises. I know that when the legal tenders were first issued, in February, 1862, we were under a dire necessity. The doubt that prevented several influential Senators, like Fessenden and Collamer, from voting for the legal tender clause, was that they were not convinced that our necessities were so extreme as to demand the issue of irredeemable paper money. Most of those who voted for it justified their vote upon the ground that the very existence of the country depended upon its ability to coin into money its promises to pay. That was the position taken by me. We were assured by Secretary Chase that nearly one hundred millions of unpaid requisitions were lying upon his table, for money due to soldiers in the presence of the enemy, and for food and clothing to maintain them at the front. We then provided for the issue of legal tender United States notes,

UNCLE SAM RESUMES SPECIE PAYMENTS

as an extreme remedy in the nation's peril. It has always seemed strange that so large and respectable a body of our fellow-citizens should regard the continuance of irredeemable money as the permanent policy of a nation so strong and rich as ours, able to pay every dollar of its debts on demand, after the causes of its issue had disappeared. To resume is to recover from illness, to escape danger, to stand sound and healthy in the financial world, with our currency based upon the intrinsic value of solid coin.

Therefore I say, may resumption be perpetual. To wish otherwise is to hope for war, danger and national peril, calamities to which our nation, like others, may be subject, but against which the earnest aspiration of every patriot will be uttered.

EDISON'S ELECTRIC LIGHT INVENTION

By Frank L. Dyar and Thomas C. Martin

OCTOBER 21, 1879, was a red-letter day in the history of electrical invention and development. On that day the incandescent lamp was brought into existence by Thomas A. Edison, and he signalized the laboratory event by shouting, "We've got it, boys!" In their collaboration of "Edison: His Life and Inventions," from which this account is taken, by permission of Harper & Brothers, Frank L. Dyar and Thomas C. Martin tell the fascinating story of this invention.

It is the glory of Edison to have eclipsed all other inventors in discovering and applying scientific truths to a practical end. The incandescent light is undoubtedly the most used of all his inventions, and the one that required the most careful research and experimenting to perfect. Its practicability having been demonstrated in 1879, it was first publicly exhibited in 1880 and the new illumination soon achieved a remarkable success even in a most remarkable industrial age.

EDISON was familiar with the numerous but impracticable and commercially unsuccessful efforts that had been previously made by other inventors and investigators to produce electric light by incandescence, and at the time he began his experiments, in 1877, almost the whole scientific world had pronounced such an idea as impossible of fulfilment. The leading electricians, physicists, and experts of the period had been studying the subject for more than a quarter of a century, and with but one known exception had proven mathematically and by close reasoning that the "Sub-division of the Electric Light," as it was then termed, was practically beyond attainment.

Opinions of this nature have ever been but a stimulus to Edison when he has given deep thought to a subject, and has become impressed with strong convictions of possibility, and in this particular case he was satisfied that the subdivision of the electric light—or, more correctly, the subdivision of the electric current—was not only possible but entirely practicable. . . .

After having devoted several months to experimental trials of carbon, at the end of 1878 . . . he turned his attention to the platinum group of metals and began a series of experiments in which he used chiefly platinum wire and iridium wire, and alloys of refractory metals in the form of wire burners for incandescent lamps. These metals have very high fusing points, and were found to last longer than the carbon strips previously used when heated up to incandescence by the electric current, although under such conditions as were then possible they were melted by excess of current after they had been lighted a comparatively short time, either in the open air or in such a vacuum as could be obtained by means of the ordinary air-pump.

Nevertheless, Edison continued along this line of experiment with unremitting vigor, making improvement after improvement, until, about April, 1879, he devised a means whereby platinum wire of a given length, which would melt in the open air when giving a light equal to four candles, would emit a light of twenty-five candle-power without fusion. This was accomplished by introducing the platinum wire into an all-glass globe, completely sealed and highly exhausted of air, and passing a current through the platinum wire while the vacuum was being made. In this, which was a new and radical invention, we see the first step toward the modern incandescent lamp. . . .

Continuing these experiments with most fervent zeal, taking no account of the passage of time, with an utter disregard for meals, and but scanty hours of sleep snatched reluctantly at odd periods of the day or night, Edison kept his laboratory going without cessation. A great variety of lamps was made of the platinum-iridium type, mostly with thermal devices to regulate the temperature of the burner and prevent its being melted by an excess of current. The study of the apparatus for obtaining more perfect "vacua" was unceasingly carried on, for Edison realized that in this there lay a potent factor of ultimate success. About August he had obtained a pump that would produce a vacuum up to about the one-hundred-thousandth part of an atmosphere. It must be remembered that the condition necessary for maintaining this high vacuum were only made possible by his invention of the one-piece-all-glass globe, in which all the joints were hermetically sealed during its manufacture into a lamp, whereby a high vacuum could be retained continuously for any length of time.

In obtaining this perfection of vacuum apparatus, Edison realized that he was approaching much nearer to a solution of the problem. In his experiments with the platinum-iridium lamps, he had been working all the time toward the proposition of high resistance and small radiating surface, until he had made a lamp having thirty feet of fine platinum wire wound upon a small bobbin of infusible material; but the desired economy, simplicity and durability were not obtained in this manner, although at all times the burner was maintained at a critically high temperature. After attaining a high degree of perfection with these lamps, he recognized their impracticable character and his mind reverted to the opinion he had formed in his early experiments two years before—viz., that carbon had the requisite resistance to permit a very simple conductor to accomplish the object if it could be used in the form of a hair-like "filament," provided the filament itself could be made sufficiently homogeneous. As we have already seen, he could not use carbon successfully in his earlier experiments, for the strips of carbon he then employed, although they were much larger than "filaments," would not stand, but were consumed in a few minutes under the imperfect conditions then at his command.

Now, however, that he had found means for obtaining and maintaining high "vacua," Edison immediately went back to carbon, which from the first he had conceived of as the ideal substance for a burner. His next step proved conclusively the correctness of his old deductions. On October 21, 1879, after many patient trials, he carbonized a piece of cotton sewing-thread bent into a loop or horseshoe form, and had it sealed into a glass globe from which he exhausted the air until a vacuum up to one-millionth of an atmosphere was produced. This lamp, when put on the circuit, lighted up brightly to incandescence and maintained its integrity for over forty hours, and lo! the practical incandescent lamp was born. . . .

The slender, fragile, tenuous thread of brittle carbon, glowing steadily and continuously with a soft light agreeable to the eyes, was the tiny key that opened the door to a world revolutionized in its interior illumination. It was a triumphant vindication of Edison's reasoning powers, his clear perceptions, his insight into possibilities, and his inventive faculty, all of which had already been productive of so many startling, practical and epoch-making inventions. And now he had stepped over the threshold of a new art which has since become so world-wide in its application as to be an integral part of modern human experience. . . .

CIVIL SERVICE REFORM DEMANDED

By George William Curtis

CURTIS gave the best years of his useful life as an editor and publicist to bringing about civil service reform in this country. In 1871 President Grant appointed the first Civil Service Commission, with Curtis as chairman. From that time until 1883, when "a constitutional, practical and effective measure for the remedy of the abuse known as the spoils system" was adopted by Congress, Curtis fought valiantly for the "merit system."

Personally he never sought political office, though many attractive posts were offered him. He was long the chief editor of Harper's Weekly, and enhanced his reputation by establishing and conducting a department in Harper's Magazine called The Editor's Easy Chair.

This address, delivered before the American Social Science Association, in 1881, is taken from his "Orations and Addresses," by permission of Harper & Brothers.

A VITAL and enduring reform in administrative methods, although it be but a return to the constitutional intention, can be accomplished only by the commanding impulse of public opinion. Permanence is secured by law, not by individual pleasure. But in this country law is only formulated public opinion. Reform of the Civil Service does not contemplate an invasion of the constitutional prerogative of the President and the Senate, nor does it propose to change the Constitution by statute. The whole system of the Civil Service proceeds, as I said, from the President, and the object of the reform movement is to enable him to fulfil the intention of the Constitution by revealing to him the desire of the country through the action of its authorized representatives. When the ground-swell of public opinion lifts Congress from the rocks, the President will gladly float with it into the deep water of wise and patriotic action. . . .

Now, it is easy to kill weeds if we can destroy their roots, and it is not difficult to determine what the principle of reform legislation should be if we can agree upon the source of the abuses to be reformed. May they not have a common origin? In fact, are they not all bound together as parts of one system? The Representative in Congress, for instance, does not ask whether the interests of the public service require this removal or that appointment, but whether, directly or indirectly, either will best serve his own interests. The Senator acts from the same motives. The President, in turn, balances between the personal interests of leading politicians—President, Senators, and Representatives all wishing to pay for personal service and to conciliate personal influence. So also the party labor required of the place holder, the task of carrying caucuses, of defeating one man and electing another, as may be·ordered, the payment of the assessment levied upon his salary —all these are the prices of the place. They are taxes paid by him as conditions of receiving a personal favor. Thus the abuses have a common source, whatever may be the plea for the system from which they spring. Whether it be urged that the system is essential to party organization, or that the desire for place is a laudable political ambition, or that the spoils system is a logical development of our political philosophy, or that new brooms sweep clean, or that any other system is un-American—whatever the form of the plea for the abuse, the conclusion is always the same, that the minor places in the Civil Service are not public trusts, but rewards and prizes for personal and political favorites.

The root of the complex evil then is personal favoritism. This produces congressional dictation, senatorial usurpation, arbitrary removals, interference in elections, political assessments, and all the consequent corruption, degradation, and danger that experience has disclosed. The method of reform, therefore, must be a plan of selection for appointment which makes favoritism impossible. The general feeling undoubtedly is that this can be accomplished by a fixed limited term. But the terms of most of the offices to which the President and the Senate appoint, and upon which the myriad minor places in the service depend, have been fixed and limited for sixty years, yet it is during that very period that the chief evils of personal patronage have appeared. . . .

If, then, legitimate cause for removal ought to be determined in public as in private business by the responsible appointing power, it is of the highest public necessity that the exercise of that power should be made as absolutely honest and independent as possible. But how can it be made honest and independent if it is not protected so far as practicable from the constant bribery of selfish interest and the illicit solicitation of personal influence? The experience of our large public patronage offices proves conclusively that the cause of the larger number of removals is not dishonesty or incompetency; it is the desire to make vacancies to fill. This is the actual cause, whatever cause may be assigned. The removals would not be made except for the pressure of politicians. But those politicians would not press for removals if they could not secure the appointment of their favorites. Make it impossible for them to secure appointment, and the pressure would instantly disappear and arbitrary removal cease.

So long, therefore, as we permit minor appointments to be made by mere personal influence and favor, a fixed limited term and removal during that term for cause only would not remedy the evil, because the incumbents would still be seeking influence to secure reappointment, and the aspirants doing the same to replace them. Removal under plea of good cause would be as wanton and arbitrary as it is now, unless the power to remove were intrusted to some other discretion than that of the superior officer, and in that case the struggle for reappointment and the knowledge that removal for the term was practically impossible would totally demoralize the service. To make sure, then, that removals shall be made for legitimate cause only, we must provide that appointment shall be made only for legitimate cause. . . .

Mr. President, in the old Arabian story, from the little box upon the seashore, carelessly opened by the fisherman, arose the towering and haughty demon, ever more monstrous and more threatening, who would not crouch again. So from the small patronage of the earlier day, from a Civil Service dealing with a national revenue of only $2,000,000, and regulated upon sound business principles, has sprung the un-American, un-Democratic, un-Republican system which destroys political independence, honor and morality, and corrodes the national character itself. In the solemn anxiety of this hour the warning words of the austere Calhoun, uttered nearly half a century ago, echo in the startled recollection like words of doom: "If you do not put this thing down it will put you down." Happily it is the historic faith of the race from which we are chiefly sprung, that eternal vigilance is the price of liberty. It is that faith which has made our mother England the great parent of free States. The same faith has made America the political hope of the world. Fortunately, removed by our position from the entanglements of European politics, and more united and peaceful at home than at any time within the memory of living men, the moment is most auspicious for remedying that abuse in our political system whose nature, proportions and perils the whole country begins clearly to discern. The will and the power to apply the remedy will be a test of the sagacity and the energy of the people. The reform of which I have spoken is essentially the people's reform.

With the instinct of robbers who run with the crowd and lustily cry "Stop thief!" those who would make the public service the monopoly of a few favorites denounce the determination to open that service to the whole people as a plan to establish an aristocracy. The huge ogre of patronage, gnawing at the character, the honor and the life of the country, grimly sneers that the people cannot help themselves and that nothing can be done. But much greater things have been done. Slavery was the Giant Despair of many good men of the last generation, but slavery was overthrown. If the spoils system, a monster only less threatening than slavery, be unconquerable, it is because the country has lost its convictions, its courage and its common sense. "I expect," said the Yankee as he surveyed a stout antagonist, "I expect that you're pretty ugly, but I cal'late I'm a darned sight uglier." I know that patronage is strong, but I believe that the American people are very much stronger.

NORTH AMERICAN RELATIONS TO SOUTH AMERICA

By James G. Blaine, Secretary of State

BLAINE having been instrumental in bringing about the nomination, followed by the election, of James A. Garfield for the Presidency in 1880, became Secretary of State in the Garfield Cabinet. While occupying that office, his foreign policy was censured, especially because of its tendency to dictate to the Latin-American governments. His policy of intervention in the Chilian-Peruvian War was reversed by Garfield's successor, President Arthur.

Blaine wrote this letter, which is preserved among the House Executive Documents of the Forty-seventh Congress, in 1881, to H. J. Kilpatrick, United States Minister to Chili. Chili was at war with Peru and Bolivia over possession of the Atacama Desert, rich in nitrate deposits, and the Chilian army occupied Lima and Callao. Desultory fighting continued until 1883, when a treaty between Peru and Chili was signed.

THE unfortunate condition of the relations between Chili and Peru makes the mission upon the duties of which you are now entering one of grave responsibility and great delicacy. Difficult as would be any intervention of the United States under ordinary circumstances, our position is further embarrassed by the failure of the conference at Arica, undertaken at our suggestion. It is evident from the protocols of that conference that Chili was prepared to dictate and not to discuss terms of peace, and that the arbitration of the United States upon any questions of difference with the allied powers of Peru and Bolivia was not acceptable and would not be accepted by the Chilian Government. Since that time the war has closed in the complete success of Chili, and in what can scarcely be considered less than the conquest of Peru and Bolivia.

This government cannot therefore anticipate that the offer of friendly intervention in the settlement of the very serious questions now pending would be agreeable to the Government of Chili. It would scarcely comport with self-respect that such an offer should be refused, and it would be of no benefit to Peru and Bolivia that it should be offered and declined. But I am sure the Chilian Government will appreciate the natural and deep interest which the United States feels in the termination of a condition so calamitous in its consequences to the best interests of all the South American Republics. It should also know that if at any time the interposition of the good offices of this government can contribute to the restoration of friendly relations between the belligerent powers, they will, upon proper intimation, be promptly offered.

While, therefore, no instructions are given you to tender officially any advice to the Government of Chili which is unsought, you will, on such opportunity as may occur, govern your conduct and representations by the considerations to which I shall now call your attention.

Without entering upon any discussion as to the causes of the late war between Chili on the one side and Peru and Bolivia on the other, this government recognizes the right which the successful conduct of that war has conferred upon Chili; and, in doing so, I will not undertake to estimate the extent to which the Chilian Government has the right to carry its calculations of the indemnities to which it is entitled, nor the security for the future, which its interests may seem to require. But if the Chilian Government, as its representatives have declared, seeks only a guarantee of future peace, it would seem natural that Peru and Bolivia should be allowed to offer such indemnity and guarantee before the annexation of territory, which is the right of conquest, is insisted upon. If these powers fail to offer what is a reasonably sufficient indemnity and guarantee, then it becomes a fair subject of consideration whether such territory may not be exacted as the necessary price of peace.

But at the conclusion of a war avowedly not of conquest, but for the solution of differences which diplomacy had failed to settle, to make the acquisition of territory a "sine qua non" of peace is calculated to cast suspicions on the professions with which war was originally declared. . . . At this day, when the right of the people to govern themselves, the fundamental basis of republican institutions, is so widely recognized, there is nothing more difficult or more dangerous than the forced transfer of territory, carrying with it an indignant and hostile population; and nothing but a necessity proven before the world can justify it. It is not a case in which the power desiring the territory can be accepted as a safe or impartial judge.

While the United States Government does not pretend to express an opinion whether or not such an annexation of territory is a necessary consequence of this war, it believes that it would be more honorable to the Chilian Government, more conducive to the security of a permanent peace, and more in consonance with those principles which are professed by all the Republics of America, that such territorial changes should be avoided as far as possible; that they should never be the result of mere force, but, if necessary, should be decided and tempered by full and equal discussion between all the powers whose people and whose national interests are involved.

At the present moment, the completeness of the victory of Chili seems to render such a diplomatic discussion impossible. The result of the conflict has been not only the defeat of the allied armies, but the dissolution of all responsible government in Peru. . . .

An effort, and apparently a very earnest and honest one, has been made to create a provisional government, which shall gradually restore order and the reign of law. But it is obvious that for such a government to succeed in obtaining the confidence either of its own people or foreign powers, it must be allowed a freedom and force of action which cannot be exercised while Chili holds absolute possession and governs by military authority. This government, therefore, has been glad to learn from its Minister in Chili, whom you succeed, that the Chilian authorities have decided to give their support to the efforts of

Señor Calderon to establish on a steady footing a provisional government in Peru.

You will, as far as you can do so with propriety and without officious intrusion, approve and encourage this disposition on the part of the Chilian Government, and this Department will be exceedingly gratified if your influence as the representative of the United States shall be instrumental in inducing the Government of Chili to give its aid and support to the restoration of regular, constitutional government in Peru, and to postpone the final settlement of all questions of territorial annexation to the diplomatic negotiations which can then be resumed with the certainty of a just, friendly and satisfactory conclusion.

In any representation which you make, you will say that the hope of the United States is that the negotiations for peace shall be conducted and the final settlement between the two countries determined, without either side invoking the aid or intervention of any European power.

The Government of the United States seeks only to perform the part of a friend to all the parties in this unhappy conflict between South American Republics, and it will regret to be compelled to consider how far that feeling might be affected, and a more active interposition forced upon it, by any attempted complication of this question with European politics.

THE ASSASSINATION OF GARFIELD

By Theodore Clarke Smith

THIS account of Garfield's assassination, shortly after he succeeded Hayes in the Presidency, is taken from Smith's "Life and Letters of James Abram Garfield," published by the Yale University Press. The author is at this writing professor of American history at Williams College, of which President Garfield was a graduate and to which he was on his way to attend his class reunion when he was shot, July 2, 1881.

The assassin, Charles J. Guiteau, was an office-seeker whose vanity had been wounded by the refusal of a government post, and whose unbalanced brain had been excited by contemporary dissensions in the Republican party. The crime excited the horror and sympathy of all parties alike; and foreign nations joined in mourning. Garfield had been removed from Washington to Elberon, New Jersey, and died there September 19, 1881. Guiteau was hanged in the jail at Washington, June 30, 1882.

ON July 2, at twenty minutes past nine o'clock, as President Garfield, accompanied by Blaine, entered the Pennsylvania Railroad station in Washington, to begin his journey to Williamstown for his class reunion, a man stepped forward and fired two pistol shots at him, each of which took effect, one grazing the arm, the other striking him in the back near the spine. The President fell under the shock, momentarily unconscious, but after an instant of stunned amazement some of the bystanders carried him to an office room in the building while others seized the assassin. The members of the Cabinet, Hunt, Windom, James and their families, who had already entered the train were hastily recalled and, with Harry and James Garfield, who had entered the station shortly after the shots were fired, assumed charge of the situation.

The first impression was that the wound was a fatal one. The injured man, not bleeding profusely but "presenting the appearance of perfect collapse," was removed from the station to the White House, where various doctors, hastily summoned by different persons, gathered in consultation. From the symptoms it was generally agreed that Garfield was undergoing internal hemorrhage and could not survive the night. It later appeared that the signs of collapse were due to the fact that the bullet had struck the spinal column, torn through part of it, although without actually touching the spinal cord, and had inflicted a violent shock upon the whole nervous system. Under the circumstances the members of the Cabinet promptly notified the Vice-President, Arthur, that he ought to be ready to take the oath of office at any minute and on the following day, the third, he arrived in Washington to wait until the outcome should be known. During the rest of the day the group of physicians did little more than watch the symptoms, after a rather superficial examination of the wound, and give stimulants under the impression that any operation to extract the ball would certainly be fatal, merely accelerating what appeared to be the rapidly approaching end.

During these hours Garfield himself was for the most part conscious and, as the bulletins said, was "mentally clear, conversing intelligently when permitted to do so." From persons who were with the crowd around him at the station or who followed to the White House have come reports showing that at this crisis his steadiness of soul stood perfectly unshaken. Garfield was always a man of marked physical courage and not even the shock of an apparently fatal bullet wound and the idea of approaching death could unnerve him. As he lay at the station before the doctors arrived he said, "I don't think this is serious," and later remarked, "I will live." Whatever his physical suffering he immediately assumed and maintained an attitude of unshaken hopefulness. At the same time he did not hesitate to face facts. One of the doctors told him plainly that he probably had internal hemorrhage. "The President," said the doctor, "replied, 'I am very glad to know my condition. I can bear it.' These words were spoken as calmly and peacefully as anything I ever heard in my life." . . .

During the night which followed, the expected collapse did not occur and by morning, to the surprise of the surgeons and the joy of the whole country, the patient was visibly rallying. Hope now returned and the situation was taken in hand with new determination. "The President," in the language of the official bulletin, "was cheerful, gave evidence of having rested and made definite inquiries regarding his condition and prospects." Less formally, one of the doctors described what happened.

"At this time he inquired of me what his chances of recovery were, saying, in his bright and cheerful way, that he desired a frank and full statement,—that he was prepared to die, and feared not to learn the worst. He added that personally he was willing to lay down the heavy burden thrust upon him. I replied, 'Mr. President, your injury is formidable. In my judgment you have a chance for recovery.' He placed his hand upon my arm and, turning his face more fully toward me, said with a cheerful smile: 'Well, Doctor, we will take that chance.' " Before night these words were telegraphed all over the United States, evoking tears of sympathy and pride at the indomitable courage and steadiness that lay behind them.

Garfield now selected Dr. D. W. Bliss, an old boyhood neighbor on the Western Reserve, considered the leading authority in Washington, to assume charge of the case and choose his associates. Dr. Bliss, who had been acting hitherto on the invitation of the Secretary of War, joined with him two army surgeons, Surgeon-General J. K. Barnes and Dr. J. J. Woodward, U.S.A., and Dr. Robert Reyburn, a local surgeon. He also sent for the two leading surgeons of Philadelphia and New York, respectively, Drs. D. H. Agnew and F. H. Hamilton. This group then made as close a study of the situation as the wound would allow and came to the conclusion that the bullet, hitting first the vertebral column and then two ribs and being deflected in an unknown direction, was not to be located; but that this was comparatively unimportant, since none of the symptoms indicated that any important internal organ had been penetrated or even badly bruised. It was agreed not to attempt an operation, in default of precise knowledge of the location of the bullet, but to adopt a waiting policy, hoping to maintain the patient's strength and to meet any indications of infection as they arose. Hence from July 3 the situation became one of careful nursing and feeding, with surgical intervention only in case of grave necessity.

Then the battle began and the White House was made into a hospital. The wives of the members of the Cabinet—Mrs. Blaine, Mrs. Windom, Mrs. Hunt, Mrs. James and Mrs. McVeagh—had acted as volunteer nurses during the first day and night, but their places were now taken by Dr. Susan Edson, a woman of middle age who had been an army nurse and was well acquainted with the Garfield family, and by Steward Crump of the White House staff, who proved surprisingly efficient and sympathetic. Room 17 was used for a while, but later room 18, a corner room, was selected as the sickroom and every possible effort made to secure coolness and quiet. The former was finally attained through a refrigerating device which furnished cool and dry air. . . .

Meanwhile the progress of the case showed clearly that infection was at work, although for weeks it seemed to make no headway. Bulletins grew more and more hopeful, until by July 13, the surgeons announced, "His gradual progress toward complete recovery is manifest and thus far without serious complications." On July 23, however, a sharp rise in temperature and a chill showed that appearances had been too favorable. An operation became necessary to open up a pus cavity which, as the report said, "must have come from a deep-seated source." This gave relief and again the daily bulletins became hopeful. After a few weeks the hope that the opening of this cavity would serve to furnish an escape for all infection was suddenly upset when on August 14 there was an attack of vomiting, rise of temperature and subsequent collapse. Just as this seemed to be passing off, there appeared a swelling in the neck, in the parotid gland, August 18; a grave symptom since it showed that infection was burrowing around in the patient's system. Ultimately the diseased gland discharged through the mouth and then the ear. The question was now raised whether the constant rise and fall of fever might not be due to malaria, rather than infection. This the surgeons were obliged to deny.

During the last part of August the situation was recognized to be grave, in large part because Garfield's digestion, always his weak point, seemed unable to surmount the difficulties in its way and failed constantly to furnish the necessary nourishment. Additional incisions had to be made in the parotid swelling. Clearly pus was forming in various places. On August 26 and 27 the doctors felt that the situation was practically hopeless. Members of the Cabinet were told that death was not far off and Arthur was again notified. Newspapers printed Washington reports under the heading, "The end expected." But the patient, with astonishing vitality, rallied from this depressed state and during the first part of September there was again hope. On the sixth, to satisfy Garfield's deep desire to escape from Washington, he was moved from his sickroom to a cottage on the New Jersey coast at Elberon. The transfer was carried out successfully, by moving his cot to a large express wagon, then placing it in a special car and having a train carry it at high speed across Maryland, Delaware, part of Pennsylvania and New Jersey. Once installed in his new room he seemed to improve, after recovering from the exhaustion and excitement of the journey, and by September 13 he was sitting up for short periods and watching the ocean with delight. "Thank God, it is good to be here," was his heartfelt remark, on smelling the salt air. . . .

At Elberon, the sea air and the coolness made Garfield fancy that he was gaining ground and on September 8, at his desire, three of the six surgeons retired from the case, leaving Drs. Bliss, Hamilton and Agnew. . . .

. . . On the seventeenth of September a visible change for the worse occurred with "a sharp rigor" and the next two days passed with increased fever, fluttering pulse and partial loss of consciousness.

THE ASSASSINATION OF GARFIELD 249

While there did not seem to be any symptoms more serious in themselves than those which had appeared a month before, the terribly emaciated and wasted condition of the patient's body made the situation almost hopeless.

All knew that the end could not be far off. On September 18 Garfield asked Rockwell, "Old boy, do you think my name will have a place in history?" The colonel answered: "Yes, a grand one, but a grander one in human hearts. Old fellow, you mustn't talk in that way. You have a great work yet to perform." After a moment's silence, he said sadly and solemnly, "No, my work is done." Yet when husband and wife met, each for the other's sake was calm and smiling. Of Mrs. Garfield, a Philadelphia paper said, "The very brightest spot in all that household has been the courage, fortitude and hope of this very remarkable woman."

On the night of September 19, the anniversary of the Battle of Chickamauga, at the hour when, eighteen years before, Garfield had been writing for Rosecrans the dispatches summoning the corps commanders to their last council before the fateful second day's fighting, the blow fell. Only the attendant and Colonel Swaim were with him when he woke and under the hand of death, for the first and only time cried out, "How it hurts here!" pressing his hand upon his heart. Swaim sprang forward, offering a drink of water, which he drained, but he immediately cried again, "Swaim, can't you stop this? O Swaim!" and became unconscious. Dr. Bliss came promptly and was followed by Mrs. Garfield, who instantly saw that the end had come, the sight extorting from her the single complaint which passed her lips, "O why am I made to suffer this cruel wrong?" Thereafter she held his hand in silence. Dr. Bliss's record of the case, breaking for the first and only time from its conventional professional wording ended thus, "Applying my ear over the heart, I detected an indistinct fluttering which continued until 10:35 when he expired. The brave and heroic sufferer, the nation's patient, for whom all had labored so cheerfully and unceasingly, had passed away."

THE BLAINE-CLEVELAND CAMPAIGN

By Harry Thurston Peck

PROFESSOR PECK, from whose "Twenty Years of the Republic" (1885-1905) this account of the memorable Blaine-Cleveland Presidential campaign of 1884 is taken, by permission of Dodd, Mead & Company, was long a member of the faculty of Columbia University and was editor of the New International Encyclopedia, as well as of a popular "Dictionary of Literature and Antiquities."

As here set forth, the defeat of Blaine, the Republican, by Cleveland, the Democratic candidate, was largely attributable to the impolitic speech of the Rev. Samuel D. Burchard in which the Democratic party was styled "the party of Rum, Romanism and Rebellion." In an unusually bitter campaign the combined Democratic and "mugwump" vote elected Cleveland, who received 219 electoral votes to 182 cast for Blaine, and was inaugurated March 4, 1885, the first Democratic President since the Civil War.

THE nomination of James G. Blaine produced an indescribable sensation throughout the length and breadth of the United States. No American statesman had ever had more ardent and intensely loyal friends than he, as none had ever had more virulent and bitter enemies. The former hailed his candidacy with intense enthusiasm; the latter began at once moving heaven and earth to compass his defeat.

Mr. Blaine had already enjoyed a remarkable career. Born in Pennsylvania of Scotch-Irish parentage, he had been by turns a teacher and an editor, having taken up in 1854 his residence in Maine. In 1858 he had entered the State Legislature, where for two years he served as Speaker. In 1862 he was sent to Congress, and at once made his mark by his readiness in debate, his quick grasp upon political principles, and his exceptional fertility in resource. He had the impetuosity of the Celt and the clear reasoning brain of the Anglo-Saxon, besides that indescribable quality which, for want of a better name, is known as magnetism. His personal charm was indeed remarkable, and it was to this as much as to his other gifts that he owed the extraordinary devotion of his followers and friends. Early in his political life he had been compared to Henry Clay, to whose career his own was to exhibit a striking parallel. At first he was better known to his associates in Congress than to the country as a whole; but when, in 1869, he was elected Speaker of the House, he rose at once to the rank of a great party leader. . . .

. . . But the fierce white light which beats upon a throne is no more fierce than that which beats upon a Presidential aspirant. It was turned at once upon Mr. Blaine's whole past career. Every incident and every act of his were now subjected to minute investigation by his enemies and rivals. A dozen stories grew until they filled the minds of every one about him. It was said that Mr. Blaine had pledged a number of worthless railroad bonds to the Union Pacific Railway Company in return for a loan of $64,000 which had never been repaid. It was also charged that without consideration he had received bonds of the Little Rock and Fort Smith Railroad. . . .

These reports obtained so widespread a currency that Mr. Blaine was forced to rise in his place and bring the matter to the attention of the House. He read a letter from the treasurer of the Union Pacific and from Colonel Thomas A. Scott, the president of that railway, denying the story of the worthless bonds. He read another letter from Morton, Bliss & Company, who were alleged to have cashed the draft for $64,000, mentioned in the story, but who now declared that no such draft had been presented to them. Mr. Blaine went on to say that he had never owned the Little Rock and Fort Smith bonds which he was said to have received without any consideration. Apparently his name was cleared.

The time for the National Republican Convention was drawing near. Many States had already instructed their delegates to support his candidacy. That he should be the subject of an investigation for corrupt transactions while his name was before the Convention would be fatal to his chances; and he desired above all things to stave it off. Nevertheless, the House, which was strongly Democratic, ordered its Judiciary Committee to make such an investigation, though in the resolution ordering it, Mr. Blaine was not specifically named. This was on May 2d; and at the first sessions of the committee the evidence was corroborative of Mr. Blaine's assertions.

On May 31st there was brought before the committee a man named James Mulligan. Mulligan had at one time been a clerk for Mr. Jacob Stanwood (the brother of Mrs. Blaine), and later a bookkeeper for Warren Fisher, Jr., a business man of Boston, who had had close relations with the management of the Little Rock and Fort Smith Railroad. While Mr. Mulligan was testifying, he chanced to mention very quietly that he had in his possession certain letters written by Mr. Blaine to Warren Fisher, Jr. Mr. Blaine asked a friend on the committee to move an immediate adjournment. The committee rose, to meet again the following morning. When it so met it listened to a most extraordinary story.

During the brief respite given by the adjournment of the committee, Mr. Blaine had flashed his mind over all the possibilities of the situation. He knew that Mulligan had letters, which, if made public by Mulligan himself, would be interpreted by every one in a sense extremely unfavorable to Mr. Blaine. He knew that these letters would surely be asked for by the committee so soon as it should reconvene in the morning. To prevent this and to gain time he must act at once. He therefore went to the Riggs House, where Mulligan was staying, and met Mulligan, Fisher and one Atkins. There he first asked to see the letters which Mulligan had with him. . . .

On June 5th, Mr. Blaine rose in the House of Representatives and claimed the floor on a question of privilege. . . . Throughout this animated and even fiery justification of his right, the crowded House had listened in breathless silence, and with a tension of feeling which could almost be felt. There was abundant sympathy with Mr. Blaine. Even his adversaries were sorry for him. He seemed like a man driven into a corner and fighting for his very life. After a brief pause, Mr. Blaine dealt a master-stroke which he had planned with consummate art, and which he now delivered with a dramatic power that was thrilling. Raising his voice and holding up a packet, he went on:

"I am not afraid to show the letters. Thank God Almighty, I am not afraid to show them! There they are. There is the very original package. And, with some sense of humiliation, with a mortification that I do not pretend to conceal, with a sense of outrage which I think any man in my position would feel, I invite the confidence of forty-four millions of my countrymen while I read those letters from this desk."

The tension was broken. The whole assembly burst out into frantic and prolonged applause. Then Mr. Blaine read the letters, one by one, with comments and explanations of his own. Having done so, he faced one of the Democratic members of the committee, Mr. Proctor Knott, and in the course of a rapid dialogue brought out the fact that Mr. Knott had received a cablegram from a Mr. Caldwell, whose knowledge of the whole affair was very intimate, and that Mr. Knott had apparently suppressed it. The scene at the end of this exciting parliamentary duel baffled all description. The House went mad; and for fifteen minutes there reigned a pandemonium amid which the Speaker was helpless in his efforts to restore even a semblance of order. Mr. Blaine, for the moment, had won a brilliant triumph. He had restored and strengthened the faith of all his followers and had turned apparently inevitable disaster into victory. . . .

The famous Mulligan letters sufficed to prevent Mr. Blaine's nomination for the Presidency in 1876 and 1880, and now, in 1884, from the outset of his candidacy, were printed and scattered broadcast over the country by his political opponents. . . .

The Democratic candidate against whom Mr. Blaine had now to make his fight was a man of a wholly antithetical type. Mr. Cleveland was in no respect a brilliant man. The son of a clergyman, and early left to make his own way in the world, he had, like his rival, been a teacher, and had later taken up the practice of the law in Buffalo. There he had held some minor public offices. In 1863 he was Assistant District Attorney for the county, and from 1870 to 1873 he had served as Sheriff. He first attracted attention outside of his own city when, in 1881, he was elected Mayor of Buffalo by a combination of Democrats and Independents. In this office he instituted reforms and defeated various corrupt combinations, while his liberal use of the veto power maintained a wise economy. In 1882 he had received the Democratic nomination for the governorship of New York, and had been elected by the remarkable plurality of 192,000 votes.

THE BLAINE-CLEVELAND CAMPAIGN

Mr. Cleveland was a type of man such as had not before come to the front as a Presidential possibility. He represented the practical, everyday, usual citizen of moderate means, and no very marked ambitions— a combination of the business man and the unimportant professional person, blunt, hardheaded, brusque, and unimaginative, and with a readiness to take a hand in whatever might be going on. His education was of the simplest, his general information presumably not very large; and his interest in life was almost wholly bounded by the limits of his own locality. As a practicing lawyer he was well thought of; yet his reputation had not gone much beyond the local circuit. A bachelor, he had no need of a large income. His spare time was spent with companions of his own tastes. His ideal of recreation was satisfied by a quiet game of pinochle in the backroom of a respectable beer-garden; and perhaps this circumstance in itself is sufficient to give a fair notion of his general environment. He was, indeed, emphatically a man's man—"homo inter homines"—careless of mere forms, blunt of speech, and somewhat primitive in his tastes.

But he had all the virile attributes of a Puritan ancestry. His will was inflexible. His force of character was extraordinary. He hated shams, believed that a thing was either right or wrong, and when he had made up his mind to any course of action, he carried it through without so much as a moment's wavering. So great was the confidence which his character inspired, that when a committee of the independent voters of Buffalo called upon him for the purpose of urging him to stand for the mayoralty, they asked him for no written pledges, but accepted his simple statement as an adequate guarantee. "Cleveland says that if elected he will do so-and-so," they told the people. And the people elected him, because they knew his word to be inviolable.

As Governor, Mr. Cleveland entered upon a wider field and one that must have seemed at first a place of limitless exactions. But his lack of imagination stood him in good stead. He bent his back to the burden and did each day's work as it came. A stranger to large responsibilities, and retaining much of the narrowness of the provincial business man, he viewed all questions as equally important, attending personally to all his correspondence, looking for himself into every item and detail of executive business, and giving hours of time each day to minutiæ which the merest clerk could have cared for with quite as much efficiency. This, however, was only one manifestation of the conscientiousness that showed itself far more commendably in higher matters. The rough, blunt independence of the man made him indifferent to the insidious influences that rise like a malarial mist about the possessor of high political office.

Subtleties of suggestion were lost on this brusque novice, and anything more pointed than suggestion roused in him a cross-grained spirit that brooked no guidance or control. He forged ahead in his own way

THE BLAINE-CLEVELAND CAMPAIGN 259

with a sort of bull-necked stubbornness, but with a power and energy which smoother politicians were compelled to recognize as very real. He cared nothing for popularity. He vetoed a bill requiring the street railways to reduce their fares, thereby offending thousands. He followed it up by a veto of another bill which granted public money to sectarian schools; and in consequence he estranged great masses of his Catholic supporters. He defied the Tammany leaders in the Legislature, and made still more powerful enemies. . . . In the end, his record as Governor of New York secured for him the nomination for the Presidency. Against the brilliant, subtle, and magnetic Blaine was pitted the plodding, incorruptible, courageous Cleveland.

The campaign opened immediately after the two candidates had been nominated. Those Republicans who were opposed to Mr. Blaine formed an organization at a conference held in New York on July 22d, and prepared an address which was issued on the 30th by the so-called National Committee of Republicans and Independents, of which George William Curtis was the chairman, and George Walton Green the secretary. At once the movement assumed formidable proportions, and it was seen that thousands of Republicans were rallying to Cleveland, not because they had given up their party, but because they could not tolerate their party's candidate. Among them were men who had been identified with the Republican party from its earliest years—Henry Ward

Beecher, William Everett, George Ticknor Curtis, Carl Schurz and James Freeman Clarke. These Independents received the popular name of "Mugwumps," a word which, having been first employed in a semi-political sense by the Indianapolis "Sentinel" in 1872, gained its popular currency through the New York "Sun," which began using it on March 23, 1884. These "Mugwumps," or political purists, had been described by Mr. Blaine four years earlier in a letter to General Garfield, in which he said: "They are noisy but not numerous; pharisaical but not practical; ambitious but not wise; pretentious but not powerful." This sentence was extremely characteristic of the man who wrote it. . . .

As the campaign proceeded, its tone became almost frantic. Those who clung loyally to Mr. Blaine did so with a passionate intensity that made them quite incapable of reasoning. The attacks on Mr. Cleveland had filled his followers with bitterest resentment. . . .

Political discussion, indeed, rapidly degenerated into personal abuse. Even the cartoonists of the different parties showed none of the humor which is usually to be found in the pictorial history of a campaign. Some of the caricatures were frightful in their malignity. . . .

Late in October it became evident that the vote of New York would decide the result of the election; and both parties concentrated upon that State their intensest energies. Mr. Cleveland as Governor had, as already described, offended the labor vote, the Roman Catholics, and Tammany Hall—three immensely powerful elements. Mr. Blaine, on the other hand, because of his Irish descent, his Catholic mother, and his professed sympathies with the cause of Ireland and the so-called Irish "patriots," was strong precisely where Cleveland was known to be most vulnerable. Yet in New York Mr. Blaine had made one venomous and implacable enemy. This was Roscoe Conkling, with whom, so far back as 1866, there had been established something like a personal feud. The two men had always been temperamentally antipathetic. Conkling was overbearing, proud of his personal appearance, and bore himself with a swagger which impressed the galleries of the House, but which was offensive even to many of his own party associates. . . .

It was Conkling who aided in preventing Blaine's nomination in 1876 and in 1880. It was Blaine, who, as Garfield's Secretary of State, urged the President to defy the New York Senator and indirectly to secure his retirement into private life. Now it was Conkling's turn again, and he meant to feed his resentment to the full. His power in New York was great, and the Republican managers could do nothing with him. . . .

Blaine, therefore, took the stump himself and went about speaking to great crowds, and endeavoring to win them by that eloquence and charm of manner which had made him famous. He was, however, no longer the indomitable political gladiator of past years. The strain of the conflict had told on him severely. Though he let it be known to few, he was acutely sensitive to the attacks that were made upon him so unscrupulously and often so brutally. He suffered even when he seemed externally serene. Moreover, his fellow candidate, General Logan, was not at all the associate whom Mr. Blaine would personally have chosen. Logan represented the opposing or "stalwart" faction of the Republican party, and was in sympathy with Conkling and his friends. . . .

Mr. Blaine had also well-nigh reached the point of physical exhaustion. His health was already undermined. His vitality was failing. As he was dragged about from place to place, stared at by mobs, having always to appear affable and interested while haunted by a premonition of disaster, he almost experienced physical collapse. The acuteness of his mind must likewise have been somewhat dulled; for when, on October 29th, a few days before the election, he received at the Fifth Avenue Hotel in New York City a number of clergymen, he failed to notice a remark of one of them who made a brief address. This clergyman was the Rev. Dr. Samuel D. Burchard, who closed his speech with the following sentence: "We are Republicans, and we do not propose to leave our party and identify ourselves with the party of Rum, Romanism and Rebellion!"

These last words, so blazingly indiscreet when publicly addressed to a candidate who hoped to carry the

THE BLAINE-CLEVELAND CAMPAIGN 263

pivotal State of New York by the aid of Catholic voters, were heard by Mr. Blaine, but their significance was not instantly appreciated. As he afterward told his friends in private conversation, he was at the moment preoccupied in thinking over the answer which he was to make. He therefore took no notice of Dr. Burchard's peroration, though it must have been personally offensive to him as the son of a Catholic mother. He had, besides, himself just returned from visiting his sister, who was the Mother Superior of a convent in Indiana.

Yet it was only after the delegation had withdrawn that he fully realized the serious blunder that he had made. He took immediate steps to suppress the word "Romanism" in the reports that were to appear in friendly newspapers. But it was too late. The Horatian maxim "Volat irrevocabile verbum," was to find a striking illustration of its truth. In less than twenty-four hours every Democratic paper in the country had spread before its readers the Burchard alliteration. Every Catholic voter in the State had read it upon handbills, and had been told that Mr. Blaine had allowed a slur upon his own mother's faith to pass unrebuked. . . .

Still, the result seemed doubtful. Tammany Hall had not yet been won over. Its leader was John Kelly, a rough and ready politician, but an honest man, according to his lights. He had opposed Mr. Cleveland's nomination, pronouncing him no Democrat, and declaring that if elected he would prove a traitor to the party. Kelly held in his control the vote of Tammany Hall; and, as a last resort, Mr. Hendricks was summoned from Indiana to exert his influence. He made the journey of a thousand miles and conferred with Kelly until at a late hour of the night. Hendricks was a party man of the straightest type, an old-time Democrat of the Middle West. He carried his point, and Kelly promised that for Hendricks's sake the Tammany vote should be cast for the party ticket.

Then came the day of the election on November 4th. Early on the following morning it was known that Cleveland had carried all the Southern States, besides New Jersey, Connecticut and Indiana. New York was still in doubt, but it seemed to have gone Democratic. The New York "Sun," which had supported the farcical Greenback candidacy of General B. F. Butler, and which was bitterly opposed to Cleveland, conceded his election. The "Tribune," on the other hand, kept its flag still flying, and declared that Blaine had won. It was evident that the result depended upon a few hundred votes in the outlying counties of New York. A very ugly feeling was manifested among the Democrats. They suspected that a plot was on foot to cheat them of their rights and to repeat the discreditable history of 1876. . . .

Mobs filled the streets in the vicinity of the newspaper offices, watching intently every bulletin that was posted, and from time to time breaking out into savage cheers or groans. Violence was attempted in several cities, and bodies of men marched up and down as they had done at the outbreak of the Civil War. The excitement was most intense in the city of New York, where it was believed that Jay Gould, who controlled the Western Union Telegraph Company, was leagued with the more unscrupulous of the Republican managers to tamper with the delayed returns. An angry mob marched to the Western Union Building with shouts of "Hang Jay Gould!" Gould besought police protection; and then dispatched a telegram of congratulations to Cleveland.

On the evening of the 18th of November, the official count was ended; and then the country knew that a plurality of 1,149 votes in the State of New York had given the Presidency to Cleveland, whose election marked an epoch in our national history, the importance of which can only now be fully understood. It meant that, with the exception of the negro question, the issues springing from the Civil War had been definitely settled. It meant the beginning of a true reunion of all States and sections. It meant that the nation had turned its back upon the past, and was about to move forward with confidence and courage to a future of material prosperity, and to a greatness of which no one at that time could form an adequate conception. And it meant, although none then surmised it, that, as a result of new conditions, there was ultimately to be effected a momentous change in the whole social and political structure of the American Republic.

THE DEATH AND FUNERAL OF GENERAL GRANT

By General James Grant Wilson

IN his "Life of General Grant," published by D. Appleton & Company, General Wilson thus recounts the death and funeral of the great Civil War commander and eighteenth President of the United States. Grant died at Mount McGregor, near Saratoga, New York, July 23, 1885, and his body rests in a magnificent tomb overlooking the Hudson River from Riverside Drive, New York City.

Wilson served under Grant in the Civil War and was brevetted brigadier-general. After the war he lived in New York and was president of the New York Genealogical and Biographical Society. He was a prolific author and editor of history and biography. In the summer of 1884 General Grant entered upon a long period of suffering from a cancerous affection of the throat. Until a few days before his death he was diligently engaged in writing his memoirs, in order to make provision for his family.

EARLY in the summer of 1884 the General began to feel a slight pain in his mouth and throat, which increased and developed into cancer of the tongue —a painful and incurable disease. As he gradually grew weaker, the whole nation watched with solicitude the progress of his malady, and prayers were offered in many pulpits in the land for his recovery; day after day expressions of sympathy came not only from all quarters of our own country, but from distant lands. Old strifes and enmities were all forgotten in the presence of approaching death, and the Blue and the Gray alike uttered the warmest expressions of sympathy for the dying soldier. Early in the month of

April there was a marked improvement in General Grant's condition, and, among some of his more sanguine friends, hopes were entertained and expressed of his ultimate recovery. Through the length and breadth of the land the morning and evening journals contained daily bulletins of one or more columns concerning the condition of the illustrious patient, and many of the leading papers of Great Britain and other lands published daily telegrams. . . .

Fortunately his prayer was answered that he might be permitted to live to complete his Military Memoirs, which were substantially finished. It may be doubted if any book has been written under similar conditions since the world began. It far surpasses Sir Walter Scott's gallant efforts to maintain the integrity of his character, that he might bequeath an untarnished name and a fantastic mansion to a long line of Scotts of Abbotsford. Seeing the last enemy approach, the dying but undaunted soldier, suffering almost constant, and at times the severest agony, determined to "fight it out" bravely as he did when he faced General Lee in the Wilderness struggle. This Grant did, to the general astonishment of publishers, physicians, family and friends, the fruit of this great effort being a fortune for his family. It was probably the most successful expensive book ever issued—more than a quarter of a million copies having been ordered in advance of publication, and nearly half a million of dollars having been received as copyright. In clearness and accuracy of statement, in literary style and finish, it compares favorably with the models of English literature.

The General, contrary to the expectations of his physicians and friends, survived to see the twentieth anniversary of the surrender of Lee's army, and to exchange greetings with his family on the return of the anniversary which may be said to have substantially broken the Confederacy and closed the four years' civil conflict. He survived to see the sun rise on the twenty-fourth anniversary of the surrender of Fort Sumter and the commencement of the war, living also to see the anniversary of the death of President Lincoln, which General Grant deemed the darkest day of his life. After more than a month's confinement to his house, he recovered sufficiently to drive out in the park again on Monday, April 20th, and on the following day he was seen walking in Sixty-sixth Street with one of his sons. About this time he was able to resume his literary work by dictating to a secretary.

He survived to complete substantially his military autobiography, by far the most valuable contributions yet made to the literature of the war. Owing to his increasing weakness and the warm weather, the date of his departure was anticipated by a week, and on June 16th, accompanied by his family, his physician, and attendants, he proceeded in a private car to Mount McGregor, near Saratoga, where a comfortable cottage was placed at the General's disposal for the summer by his friend, Joseph W. Drexel, of New

York, by whom it was presented after Grant's death to the Grand Army of the Republic of New York.

From his mountain home on a spur of the Adirondacks General Grant could see at a glance the great theater of the many brilliant movements of Burgoyne's campaign—his marches, his defeats, and his surrender—and the stately monument which commemorates the historic field of the grounded arms.

A few days before his departure from the city, when in a cheerful mood, the General said to a friend: "It is a great consolation to me in my sickness to know that the people, both North and South, are seemingly equally kind in their expressions of sympathy. Scores of letters come to me daily, without reference to politics or locality, containing kind words. Many communications are also received from public bodies. But nothing has touched me more deeply than the daily spectacle of the crowds of people gathering about my door for months, and eagerly seeking information as to my condition. Yes, I can certainly say that I tried to do my duty to my country, and I hope I have always treated those who were not on the same side with me, both in the field and in politics, with justice. The men of the South I always looked upon as citizens of our common country, and when it was in my power I always treated them as such. I can say with truth that I never, even in the midst of duty, had any other feeling than that which one citizen should feel toward another." The General also referred with much feeling to the many kind schemes projected in his behalf by friends in California and in other portions of the country.

The ex-President's prayer that the end would come soon was granted, but not before the wish nearest to his heart was gratified—that he should live to finish his book. After many temporary rallies and improvements and much physical suffering, borne in the spirit of Paul's grand text—"Endure hardness as a soldier" —surrounded by all those who were near and dear to him, the illustrious commander passed away peacefully at eight minutes past eight on Thursday morning, July 23, 1885.

More than royal honors may be said to have been paid to his memory by the messages of condolence which came to Mrs. Grant from crowned heads and from distinguished personages of various countries and climes. It was the absorbing topic with the press and people of the United States during the period that elapsed between the time of the illustrious soldier's death and burial. Both at home and abroad he was universally recognized as the First Soldier and the First Citizen of the New World. Against this compact consensus of opinion there was no discordant voice, even among the people against whom he wielded his mighty sword. The men of the South had only words of praise for their generous conqueror. . . .

Before his death General Grant expressed in writing a wish that he should be buried in one of three places—at West Point, where he received his education, in Illinois, where he resided for several years, or in New York, "because the people of that city befriended me in my need." New York, through its Mayor, having proffered to Mrs. Grant a burial place in any of the city parks, a spot was selected and accepted in Riverside Park with the single condition that, in accordance with the General's desire, his wife should hereafter be laid by his side. His preference would have been for West Point had he not been under the mistaken impression that Mrs. Grant could not be buried there.

A few days after the hero's death a large and influential committee, with ex-President Arthur as chairman, was appointed by the Mayor of New York to receive and collect funds for the erection of a national monument over General Grant's grave. Within a week of the inauguration of the movement, and before his burial, a sum of thirty thousand dollars was received by voluntary contributions. It was afterward increased to six hundred thousand dollars. Movements for other monuments throughout the country were inaugurated, and several cities of the North already possess statues of the great soldier.

On Tuesday, August 4, a memorial service was held at Mount McGregor in the cottage where Grant died, and a funeral address was delivered. On the same day, and almost at the same hour, a similar service was held in Westminster Abbey, London. The exercises were very impressive, and the vast audience which crowded the ancient abbey gave evidence of sincere sorrow and reverence for the dead soldier. The Dean of Canterbury delivered an eloquent discourse, classing General Grant with Lincoln as a statesman, and with Washington and Wellington as a strategist. Among those present were representatives of the Queen and the Prince of Wales, the Commander-in-Chief of the British Army, Mr. Gladstone, and hundreds of the most eminent statesmen and soldiers of England.

The remains of the ex-President arrived in Albany in the afternoon of the same day, and were received by the Governor. They were placed in the State Capitol, where they were seen by large numbers of citizens and people who came from the surrounding country to take their farewell view of his well-known face. On Wednesday afternoon, the 5th, the body of the great soldier arrived in New York, and was escorted by an imposing body of troops to the City Hall. For three days it lay in state, and was viewed by nearly a quarter of a million of persons, including a large number of old soldiers who had served under him.

Saturday, August 8th, was the day appointed for his public funeral, the arrangements having been made by General Winfield S. Hancock. A more magnificent demonstration was never witnessed in the New World, attesting the nation's admiration and respect for the memory of the American soldier. It is supposed that at least a million and a half persons saw the procession. The streets of the city echoed

Tomb of General Grant
Riverside Drive, New York City

to the tramp of thirty thousand soldiers and veterans who marched with measured tread to the solemn music of a hundred military bands. There were to be seen heroes of scores of battles, and the torn and tattered flags that waved over Shiloh, Vicksburg, the Wilderness, and other well-contested fields. Never but once before and once since in the history of New York have so large a number of armed men marched through its streets. . . .

It was nearly six hours after the funeral cortege left the City Hall that the catafalque, drawn by twenty-four horses, reached the grave on the banks of the historic Hudson, and was placed in the temporary tomb with appropriate ceremonies, in the presence of his family, the President of the United States, his Cabinet, ex-Presidents Hayes and Arthur, his pall-bearers, Generals Sherman and Sheridan of the Union armies, and Generals Johnston and Buckner of the Confederate service, with many of the most eminent men of the country. So, on that bright and sunny August afternoon, he was laid to rest. . . .

THE CHICAGO HAYMARKET RIOT

By Harry Thurston Peck

PECK, in his "Twenty Years of the Republic," published by Dodd, Mead & Company, gives this well-written, impartial account of the Haymarket Square tragedy of 1886, in which 8 Chicago policemen were killed and scores wounded by a bomb thrown by an anarchist, supposed to have been one Schnaubelt. As Dr. Peck states, the tragedy was the culmination of labor disturbances throughout the country, largely instigated by "preachers of violence" bent on a general seizure of property and the murder of its owners.

In Chicago a great eight-hour strike had left some 50,000 workers idle and in an ugly temper. In Haymarket Square, May 4, the bomb-throwing occurred while a mob was being harangued by such radicals as Spies, Fischer, Engel and Parsons, who were later convicted and hanged as accomplices; Fielde and Schwab, who were sentenced to life imprisonment, and Neebe, to fifteen years. Another, Lingg, committed suicide.

THE year 1886 was marked by serious disturbances arising from strikes and other labor movements, which recalled the events of 1877, when the industries of the country were paralyzed, and when, at the great centers of traffic in twelve States, conditions existed that seemed to threaten civil war. In 1886, there was less violence, yet the social unrest was so widespread as to be at once significant and ominous. From the shipyards in Maine to the railways in Texas and the Far West, there was continual disorder in nearly every branch of industry. In New York City, the employees of the street-car lines began a strike on February 3d, which was ended on the 18th by a victory for the strikers. The disturbances, however, broke out again on March 2d and continued intermittently until September 1st, when the managers of the roads once more gave way. On one day every line in New York and Brooklyn was "tied up" completely. In June, the elevated railways had a similar, though much more brief, experience. The mania for striking seemed to be in the very air; and on April 20th, in Boston, even the children in two of the public schools struck for a continuous session, and adopted all the approved methods of the conventional strike, stationing pickets, attacking such children as refused to join them, and causing a small riot which had to be put down by the police.

The storm centers of labor agitation were in St. Louis and Chicago. In St. Louis a demand was made by the employees of the Texas Pacific Railway for the reinstatement of a foreman who had been discharged. The receiver refused the demand, and a strike took place which very soon extended to the Missouri Pacific, and, in fact, to all the roads constituting the Gould system. Traffic throughout the whole Southwest was practically suspended, and before long the strike took on the form of riot and incendiarism. United States troops were sent to maintain order, but their numbers were insufficient, and the rioters cared nothing for the special deputies who had been sworn in to keep the peace. A squad of these deputies fired upon a crowd, killing or wounding a number of persons (April 7th). This act inflamed the mob, which armed itself, and for a time was master of the city.

The torch was applied to railroad property, factories were closed, and great losses were inflicted, not only upon the railways, but upon the entire population.

The leader in these depredations was a Scotchman named Martin Irons, a typical specimen of the ignorant fanatic, exactly the sort of man who comes to the front whenever the populace is inflamed by passion and bent on violence. Sly, ignorant, and half an animal, he nevertheless was able to play upon the prejudices of his fellows, and to stimulate their class-hatred so artfully as to make them deaf to the counsels of their saner leaders. For a time he had his way; yet in the end this strike collapsed after those who shared in it had forfeited hundreds of thousands of dollars in wages, and after the railroads had incurred an even heavier loss.

In Chicago, the men in the Pullman works began a strike in May; and before long nearly fifty thousand laborers were out. In a conflict with the police a number of workingmen were shot. Chicago had for some time been the headquarters of a small but very active group of anarchists, nearly all of whom were foreigners. The strikers had no sympathy with anarchists, nor any affiliation with them. Nevertheless, the anarchists believed that the proper moment had now come for them to strike a blow, and they hoped thereby to win to their support new followers from the ranks of the discontented. There were published in Chicago two newspapers, one in English (the "Alarm"), conducted by a man named Parsons, and the other in German (the "Arbeiter Zeitung"), conducted by one August Spies, both of them devoted to the anarchistic propaganda. About the time when the strike began, there appeared in the "Alarm" a most inflammatory article, of which the following is a part:

"DYNAMITE! Of all the good stuff this is the stuff. Stuff several pounds of this sublime stuff into an inch pipe, plug up both ends, insert a cap with a fuse attached, place this in the immediate neighborhood of a lot of rich loafers who live by the sweat of other people's brows, and light the fuse. The dear stuff can be carried around in the pocket without danger; while it is a formidable weapon against any force of militia, police or detectives that may want to stifle the cry for justice that goes forth from the, plundered slaves."

On May 4th, a mass-meeting of workingmen was held in the Haymarket Square to protest against the acts of the police. Late at night, after some rather tame addresses had been delivered, an anarchist leader, an Englishman named Samuel Fielde, broke forth into a violent harangue. He denounced all government in the most savage terms, yelling out, "The law is your enemy! We are rebels against it!" Word had been sent to police headquarters; and while Fielde was in the midst of his wild talk, a battalion of nearly two hundred policemen marched into the Square. Their captain commanded the gathering to disperse. Fielde replied, "We are peaceable." He was, however, arrested. A moment later, a pistol was fired, apparently as a signal, and at once a bomb was hurled into the ranks of the police. It exploded with terrible effect.

Nearly fifty policemen were thrown to the ground, and seven of them were so badly wounded that they died soon after. With splendid discipline, the ranks were at once closed up and a charge was made upon the mob, which scattered hastily in flight. Of the anarchists arrested for this outrage, seven were sentenced to death by Judge Gary. Of these seven, four —Engel, Spies, Parsons and Fischer—were hanged; one—Lingg—committed suicide, and two—Schwab and Fielde—had their sentences commuted to imprisonment for life. Eight years afterward, a Governor of Illinois, John P. Altgeld, moved partly by the appeals of sentimentalists, and partly by his own instinctive sympathy with lawlessness, gave a free pardon to such anarchists as had been imprisoned.

In June, 1886, in New York, the disturbed conditions were reflected in political agitation, though here, also, the anarchists showed their heads. They were, however, dealt with before they could do mischief. One of their leaders, named Johann Most, and three of his companions, were imprisoned on the charges of inciting a riot. . . .

Wherever throughout the country the labor element had shown its discontent, the name of the Knights of Labor was, in one way or another, pretty certain to be heard. This organization was one whose origin and evolution are of great significance in the social and economic history of the United States. Prior to 1866, such organizations of workingmen as existed were either societies for general purposes, not necessarily connected with labor questions, or else they were trade-unions in the narrowest sense, confining their membership to men and women engaged in particular and special industries. In 1866, however, there was formed the National Labor Union, of which the purpose was to promote the solidarity, not only of skilled workmen, but of the masses in general, with a view to the amelioration of their condition. This body, unfortunately, almost from the first, fell into the hands of politicians, and in 1870 it died a natural death. Its aims, however, were adopted by a number of garment-cutters in Philadelphia, in 1869, who at first formed a secret order—secrecy being adopted because of the hostility of employers to labor organizations.

This was the origin of the Knights of Labor, who admitted to membership in their body all persons above the age of sixteen, except saloon-keepers, gamblers, bankers and lawyers. In 1882, it ceased to be a secret order; and thereafter it rapidly increased in membership until, in 1886, it was said to number more than seven hundred thousand persons. The principles which the order officially professed were distinctly socialistic. It advocated equal rights for women, the common ownership of land, and the acquisition by the Government of public utilities, such as railroads, telegraphs and telephones. It is here that we first find in the United States a large and influential body of men pledged to the support of what was in reality a system of State Socialism.

In order to understand the significance of this movement, and to explain the rapid propagation of socialistic principles, it is necessary to recall a few important facts relating to American economic history of the preceding thirty years. One effect of the Civil War had been the rapid acquisition of great fortunes by individuals, and the growth of powerful corporations. Conspicuous among the latter were the railway companies. The period succeeding the war had been a period of railway building. Between 1860 and 1880 more than sixty thousand miles of railway had been constructed and put into operation. They represented an enormous amount of capital, and this capital represented an enormous amount of influence, both political and social. How much the nation owed to its railway system was very obvious. The easy distribution of its products brought prosperity to every section. Great cities sprang up in the prairies at the magic touch of the railway.

Moreover, in one sense, the unity of the Republic itself was the work of the railway, which proved to be a great assimilator, annihilating distance, bringing one section into easy communication with another, and thereby creating not only common interests, but a common understanding. On the other hand, a moment's thought will make it clear that railways were essentially monopolies, and that their growth lodged in the hands of their owners the right to tax at will the people from whom they had received their charters, and whose interests they were supposed to serve.

Even if the individuals to whom this irresponsible power was entrusted had been always wise, unselfish and public-spirited, the unregulated right of taxation would have been an anomaly in a free State. But as they were very human, serving their own interests, and naturally seeking their own enrichment, abuses, and very gross ones, were inevitable. Still, no hostile sentiment would have been aroused against them had they levied their transportation tax equitably upon all and without discrimination. That they did not do so, and that in consequence they began, about 1870, to create and foster other still more gigantic combinations inimical to the public welfare, are facts which serve to explain the prevalence throughout the country of great social discontent, beginning in 1870 and growing deeper and more intense with each succeeding year.

THE INTERSTATE COMMERCE COMMISSION

By Aldace Freeman Walker

WHEN the Interstate Commerce Commission was organized in 1887, President Cleveland appointed Walker, the author of this article which was printed in The Forum of July, 1891, a member of the body. He served on the Commission two years, subsequently holding important positions in railway traffic associations until 1894, when he became a receiver of the Atchison, Topeka & Santa Fe Railroad, and, later, chairman of the board of directors of the reorganized company.

The operation of the Interstate Commerce Act has not been all that was hoped for. The most satisfactory result of the law has been the publicity which it has given to railroad affairs. The clause of the act designed to prohibit pooling has accomplished the desired end, but has helped rather than hindered the unified management of railroads which it was designed to prevent.

ON April 5, 1887, an act of Congress became effective, bearing the comprehensive title of "An Act to Regulate Commerce." It was an entirely new departure in Federal legislation. Its authority rests upon a constitutional provision which confers upon Congress power "to regulate commerce . . . among the several States," the extent and limitations of which have never been judicially determined.

The railroads of the United States are creatures of State legislation. There has been no governmental supervision of railway construction. New lines have everywhere been authorized with the utmost freedom by the various States and Territories, and leases, purchases and consolidations have been easily arranged in which State lines have been altogether disregarded. The railroad system has been a most potent agency for the practical unification of our country by quietly obliterating territorial divisions, while threading the land with a network of iron rails along which interstate commerce moves without rest.

The course pursued in establishing the modern transportation facility has been so hasty and inconsiderate that the fundamental relation of the Nation to the several railroad corporations is to this day unsettled. . . . Competing lines have been multiplied and expanded, until their very number is now the source of the most serious practical difficulties connected with our domestic commerce.

This universal reliance upon competition as the safeguard of the public has had two noticeable results: first, it has tended to entrench railroad managers in the belief that the public was protected sufficiently thereby, and that carriers by rail, like carriers by sea, were entitled to fix rates at will, subject only to the control of competitive conditions. . . .

In the second place, in its practical working, competition bred discrimination. The evils of unjust discrimination in railway methods cannot be too vividly portrayed. As time went on they became more and more pronounced, until they were too great to be endured. Legislative investigations were demanded. . . .

The remedy proposed was the forbidding of unjust discrimination under pains and penalties. That was the essence of the Interstate Commerce law. In other words, the result was prohibited while the cause was left in full operation. It was thought that free and unrestricted competition must be maintained as an essential principle of the American railway system. . . .

. . . Of course discriminations in railway rates are necessary; for example, the rate upon silk and upon sand should not be the same, and the question is often a doubtful one whether a particular discrimination is or is not unjust. The determination of this question, arising in innumerable forms, is the matter which has chiefly occupied the attention of the Commission since the passage of the law. . . .

. . . When the law first went into operation it was felt that a new era had arrived. The statute demanded the undeviating and inflexible maintenance of the published tariff rates. . . . This was just what conservative and influential railway managers desired. It was not only just, but it protected their revenues. The new rule was cheerfully accepted and imperative orders were issued for its obedience. But toward the close of 1887 it began to be perceived that there were difficulties, which became much more serious in 1888. On even rates the traffic naturally flowed to the direct lines, which could give the best service and make the best time. Roads less direct or of less capacity, roads with higher grades or less advantageous terminals and roads otherwise at a disadvantage, found that business was leaving them. It was discovered that the law in this its most essential feature, as well as in other respects, was practically a direct interference by the government in favor of the strong roads and against the weak. Dissatisfaction arose among officials of roads whose earnings were reduced and which were often near the edge of insolvency. It had been customary for them to obtain business by rebates and other like devices, and they knew no other method. It presently became to some of them a case of desperation. There was nothing in the law specifically forbidding the payment of "commissions," and it was found that the routing of business might be secured to a given line by a slight expenditure of that nature to a shipper's friend. Other kindred devices were suggested, some new, some old; the payment of rent, clerk hire, dock charges, elevator fees, drayage, the allowance of exaggerated claims, free transportation within some single State—a hundred ingenious forms of evading the plain requirements of the law—were said to be in use. The demoralization was not by any means confined to the minor roads; shippers were ready to give information to other lines concerning concessions which were offered them, and to state the sum required to control their patronage. A freight agent thus appealed to at first perhaps might let the business go, but when the matter became more serious and he saw one large shipper after another seeking a less desirable route, he was very apt to throw up his hands and fall in with the procession.

Meanwhile nothing was done in the way of the enforcement of the law. It was found that the sixth or administrative section had been so framed as to require the exact maintenance of the tariffs of each carrier, but that this important provision had been omitted respecting "joint tariffs," in which two or more carriers participate. . . .

Toward the end of the second year came a reaching out for a remedy. In the closing days of the Fiftieth Congress amendments to the law were adopted by which shippers as well as carriers were made subject to its penalties, and the punishment of imprisonment was added to the fine in cases of unjust discrimination; joint tariffs were also distinctly brought within the jurisdiction of the Commission and the courts.

These amendments became effective March 2, 1889, and their influence was immediately felt. . . . The third year therefore exhibited an almost entire cessation of the use of illegitimate methods for securing business, and until near its close little complaint was heard. The fourth year, 1890, witnessed a renewed relaxation of the spirit of obedience. The conditions that had prevailed in 1888 again became pressing, and evasions secretly inaugurated were not efficiently dealt with; for a considerable time no prosecutions were commenced; customers began to renew their appeals for favors, or as they term it, for relief; and it was presently a common statement among shippers and traffic agents that the law was a dead letter, and that its penalties need not be feared.

THE PRESIDENTIAL CAMPAIGN OF 1888

By Edward Stanwood

ALTHOUGH Benjamin Harrison, twenty-third President of the United States, was a great-grandson of a signer of the Declaration of Independence and a grandson of William Henry (Tippecanoe) Harrison, ninth President, he was not regarded so highly as was Blaine as a Presidential possibility, on the eve of the Republican National Convention of 1888. In fact, the Republican nomination would have gone to Blaine had he not positively declared his unwillingness to accept it. Consequently the Convention, held in Chicago, nominated Harrison on the eighth ballot, and he defeated Grover Cleveland in a vigorous campaign.

His administration was characterized by a firm defense of American interests in foreign affairs and a general promotion of industry and of governmental effectiveness.

This account is taken from Stanwood's authoritative "History of Presidential Elections," by permission of the publishers, Houghton, Mifflin & Company.

SIX months before the meeting of the nominating conventions it seemed to be certain that the Presidential contest of 1888 would be between the same candidates who had been pitted against each other in 1884 — Cleveland and Blaine. The President made no public manifestation of his wish to be nominated for reëlection, but it was not necessary that he should do so. It appeared to be the wellnigh universal wish of his party that he should be again the leader of their forces, and he was understood to be entirely willing to accept the position.

On the other hand, the desire of the Republicans that Blaine should head the ticket once more found overwhelming expression among them. The unanimity of the sentiment was surprising. It is probably safe to say that had the delegates to the Convention been elected in December, 1887, there would not have been chosen a dozen in all the country who would have preferred any other candidate to Blaine. Great, therefore, was the confusion into which the party was thrown by the withdrawal of Blaine from the contest. On January 25, 1888, he addressed, from Florence, Italy, a letter to the chairman of the Republican National Committee, in which, on account of "considerations entirely personal to myself," he announced that his name would not be presented to the National Convention. At the same time he congratulated the party upon its cheering prospects, foretold that the tariff was to be the great issue of the canvass, and expressed confidence that the result could not be in doubt. Republicans were dismayed by this letter, for while they all agreed that it was a genuine and sincere refusal to accept the nomination, yet many of his friends, in the earnestness of their wish that he should be again the candidate, persuaded themselves that he would accept the mandate of the party if it were to be expressed with great unanimity. But while these excessively zealous champions persisted in their purpose to choose and send to the Convention delegates who were for Blaine, "first, last, and all the time," the acceptance of his withdrawal as a finality by the party at large resulted in the coming forward of many candidates. The unwillingness of

THE PRESIDENTIAL CAMPAIGN OF 1888

Blaine's most ardent friends to give up the hope of nominating him placed that gentleman in a position of embarrassment from which he extricated himself by a second letter, dated at Paris, May 17, in which he reiterated that he "could not accept the nomination without leaving in the minds of thousands (friends of other candidates) the impression that I had not been free from indirection, and therefore I cannot accept it at all."

Two conventions were held simultaneously in Cincinnati beginning on the 15th of May. These conventions were held by two factions of the Labor party, known respectively as the "Union Labor" and the "United Labor" parties. . . .

The National Prohibition party began its convention at Indianapolis on May 20. The gathering was a large one. It was estimated that there were at least four thousand members of the party in attendance on the convention, besides the delegates. Nearly all the States were represented and the committees on credentials reported that there were one thousand and twenty-nine delegates present. . . .

The Democrats assembled in National Convention at St. Louis on the 5th of June. Notwithstanding the certainty of Cleveland's nomination there was an enormous gathering of prominent members of the party from North and South. . . .

For the first time since 1840, when Martin Van Buren was nominated for reëlection by resolution, and not by the individual votes of delegates, there was no voting for a candidate for President. A motion was made and carried with great enthusiasm to place Grover Cleveland in nomination for a second term. The death of Vice-President Hendricks in the first year of his term had left the second place on the ticket open to a contest. Several candidates had appeared, but before the convention met the sentiment of the delegates was setting strongly in favor of Allan G. Thurman, of Ohio. . . .

The Republican Convention was held at Chicago June 19. John M. Thurston, of Nebraska, was the temporary chairman, and M. M. Estes, of California, was the permanent president. . . .

The withdrawal of Blaine, as had been explained, had left the field open for all contestants, and not only was there an unusually large number of "favorite sons," but several prominent gentlemen, who were not brought forward as candidates by the delegates representing the respective States of their residence, were mentioned as possible candidates in case the contest should be long and the difficulty of agreeing upon a nominee great. Pervading the Convention at all times, up to the moment that a nomination was effected, was a feeling that the name of Blaine might be presented in such a way, at a critical period, that the Convention would be carried away by an outburst of irrepressible enthusiasm, and that he would be summoned to lead the party again by a call so vociferous that he could not decline. Blaine gave no countenance or help to this movement. At the very opening of the Convention, having learned that some of his indiscreet friends were making unauthorized use of his name, and were assuming what he would do in certain contingencies, Blaine requested the London correspondent of the "New York Tribune" to say that all rumors "pretending to give letters or dispatches, from him or any of his party, touching political topics of any kind may be promptly discredited unless signed by Mr. Blaine himself," and, further, that he had written nothing concerning the Presidential nominations except the two published letters from Florence and Paris, and that he had held no correspondence of any kind with any one on political subjects. Even this did not prevent many men from thinking that the nomination of Blaine was the most probable outcome of the contest. Some of the delegates persisted in voting for him from first to last; and the Blaine stampede was the event which the whole country expected. But the fitting moment for it never came, and the judgment of the cooler members of the Convention was against it at all times, chiefly because they saw, what Blaine had said so clearly, that he could not honorably accept the nomination, even if it were to be thrust upon him. . . .

. . . The votes were divided among thirteen candidates, and even on the fourth trial the number had been reduced only to ten. . . .

The session of the Convention was one of the longest in the history of the country. It began on June 19. The platform was adopted on the 21st. Two votes for Presidential candidate were taken on the 22d, three on the 23d, and three on the 25th (the 24th was Sunday). The history of former Conventions was repeated; the leading candidate did not greatly increase his vote, and a concentration took place gradually upon one who had at the beginning a small but a compact and aggressive body of followers. General Benjamin Harrison, of Indiana, was nominated upon the eighth vote. . . . Levi P. Morton, of New York, was nominated for Vice-President on the first vote. . . .

The joint committee for counting the votes was held in the hall of the House of Representatives February 13, 1889. The proceedings were devoid of striking incident. . . . When the vote for Indiana was reported, the vote of the President-elect's own State, there was applause, which was quickly suppressed. Mr. Manderson, the first of the Senate tellers, reported the state of the vote in detail, and in a summary; the presiding officer repeated the summary, and added a formula, drawn from the law, that this announcement of the state of the vote "is, by law, a sufficient declaration" that Benjamin Harrison, of the State of Indiana, had been elected President, and Levi P. Morton, of the State of New York, Vice-President, for the ensuing term.

DISPUTING THE SAMOAN ISLANDS WITH GERMANY

By Harry Thurston Peck

DR. PECK gives this stirring account of the threatened conflict between the United States and Germany over the Samoan Islands, in his "Twenty Years of the Republic," published by Dodd, Mead & Company. In 1888 interests hostile to the Germans brought about the election of Mataafa as opposition King to Tamasese, and civil war broke out. While a general insurrection was in progress, with several German, British and American warships anchored in Apia roadstead, on March 16, 1889, a tidal wave and typhoon destroyed the American and German fleets. The British cruiser, Calliope, alone escaped.

Of the American vessels, the Trenton *and the* Vandalia *were sunk, and the* Nipsic *cast on shore, fifty-two officers and men being lost. Eventually the "incident" was closed by a complete American diplomatic victory, in the Act of Berlin, June 14, 1889.*

THE Samoan Islands are twelve in number, lying in the track of vessels which ply between the American seaports on the Pacific Coast and Australia. They have, therefore, a certain commercial importance, and to a naval power a definite strategic value. Upon the principal island, Upolu, where the chief town, Apia, is situated, a number of Germans, Americans and English had settled. A Hamburg trading firm was established there, besides a thriving American business house and a company of Scotch merchants. In 1878, a treaty was made by which the Samoan chief or "king" of that time gave to the United States the use of the harbor of Pago-Pago for a naval station.

As was natural, the small foreign community in Upolu, isolated from the greater world outside and thus thrown in upon itself, was rent by the small jealousies, intrigues and bickerings which arise when petty interests clash in a petty sphere. Race prejudice intensified the feeling, until Apia fairly seethed with pent-up enmities. Gradually, however, two distinct factions were formed, when the Americans and English made common cause against the Germans, who were the more numerous and who were also unpleasantly aggressive. By the year 1884, it had become clear that Germany intended by hook or by crook to get control of the Islands, and in doing so to ignore the rights of the English and American residents. The German consul, one Herr Stübel, began to manifest extreme activity. He had all the "morgue" and frigid insolence of the true Prussian official, and moreover he had at his beck several German ships of war, which always appeared most opportunely whenever Stübel was carrying things with a particularly high hand. The German residents assumed a most offensive bearing toward the other foreigners as well as toward the natives. In April 1886, Stübel raised the German flag over Apia and in a proclamation declared that only the Government of Germany should thereafter rule over that portion of the islands. The British consul hesitated to act without instructions; but the American representative hoisted the colors of the United States and proclaimed an American protectorate. This conflict of authority was serious, and

DISPUTING THE SAMOAN ISLANDS 295

led Secretary Bayard to energetic action. A conference at Washington between the representatives of Germany, Great Britain and the United States, agreed that the action of both consuls should be disavowed and that the "status quo ante" should be preserved in Samoa pending further negotiations.

Bismarck, however, had no intention of abandoning his ultimate purpose, or even of abiding by his agreement. A new consul, Herr Becker, was sent out from Berlin and proved to be as obnoxious as his predecessor. He planned a stroke that was delivered with prompt efficiency. The native king, Malietoa, was favorable to the English and Americans. Becker, seizing upon the pretext afforded by a drunken brawl between the German sailors and a few Samoans, declared war upon Malietoa, "by order of His Majesty, the German Kaiser." Martial law was proclaimed in Apia; German marines were landed; Malietoa was seized and was deported in a German ship; while a native named Tamasese, a creature of the Germans, was set up in his place. From that moment events tended rapidly toward a crisis. The American consul, Mr. Harold M. Sewall of Maine, wrote vigorous despatches to Washington and sent emphatic protests to Herr Becker, who answered him with sneering incivility. The Samoans refused to acknowledge the German puppet king and took to the bush, where the English and Americans furnished them with arms. But in Apia, a German judge was set over the local courts, the captain of a German cruiser was made

Prime Minister, and the German flag again flew over the soil which Germany had pledged itself to regard as neutral territory. A writer of genius, Mr. Robert Louis Stevenson, who was a resident of Samoa throughout these troublous times, has left a minute account of the intolerable bearing of the Germans and of the indignities to which other foreigners were subjected by them. Mr. Sewall, single-handed, resisted their aggressions. The British consul sympathized with him; but the spell of Germany's predominance in Europe seemed to paralyze his will. At last, to punish those Samoans who were in arms against Tamasese, the German corvette "Adler" was ordered to shell the native villages, and thus to inspire the people with a wholesome dread of German power.

Just prior to this time, there had arrived in Samoan waters the United States gunboat "Adams," under the orders of Commander Richard Leary. Commander Leary was to his very finger-tips a first-class fighting man. His name, as Stevenson remarked, was diagnostic. It told significantly of a strain of Celtic blood in the man who bore it. Leary had, indeed, a true Irishman's nimbleness of wit, an Irishman's love of trouble for its own sake, and even more than an Irishman's pugnacity. When he had learned just how things stood in Apia, and when he had noted the bullying demeanor of the Germans, his blood grew hot. Until now the notes of protest addressed to Becker had been couched in formal phrases. From the moment when Leary took a hand in the correspondence these notes became suddenly pungent with a malicious and most ingenious wit which made the sacrosanct emissaries of His Imperial and Royal German Majesty fairly gasp with indignation. The diabolical cleverness with which Leary followed up their every move was utterly infuriating, and no less so was his supreme indifference to what they thought or wanted. When the German warship fired rocket-signals at night, Leary used to sit on his after-deck and send up showers of miscellaneous rockets, which made the German signaling quite unintelligible. He refused to recognize their appointed king, and in a score of ways he covered them with a ridicule which seemed likely to make them ludicrous even in the natives' eyes. Meanwhile, a German night attack upon the Samoan "rebels" had been repulsed and several Germans had been killed. Very eagerly, then, did Herr Becker urge the captain of the "Adler" to bombard the "rebel" position at Apia. Surely the sound of the "Kanonendonner" would bring the natives, and also the insolent Yankees, to their senses. Captain Fritze of the "Adler" therefore ordered up his ammunition and prepared for the bombardment.

Leary's ship, the "Adams," was a wooden vessel whose heavy armament consisted of smooth-bores, only a few of which had been converted into rifled guns. The German corvette was also wooden, but her guns were of the latest pattern turned out by Krupp. Nevertheless, at short range, this superiority would count for little; and the "Adams" was commanded by a sailor who would rather fight than eat. At the appointed hour, the "Adler" steamed out with the German ensign flying at her peak. The "Adams" followed close upon her heels, as if for purposes of observation; but it was noticed that her deck was cleared for action. Soon the "Adler" slowed down and swung into position, so as to bring her broadside guns to bear upon the helpless village. Instantly volumes of black smoke poured from the funnel of the "Adams," the long roll of her drums was heard as they beat to quarters, and the American ship dashed in between the "Adler" and the shore, where she, too, swung about, her guns at port and trained directly on the Germans. Presently, Commander Leary in full uniform and accompanied by his staff boarded the "Adler." His colloquy with the German captain was short and sharp: "If you fire," said he, "you must fire through the ship which I have the honor to command. I shall not be answerable for the consequences!" So saying, he took his leave and returned to his own vessel.

Captain Fritze could scarcely believe his ears. Such audacity had never yet confronted him. He could not fire on the village unless he fired through the "Adams." He knew that his first shot would be answered by an American broadside, and that this would be the signal for a war between his country and the American Republic. He faltered, shrinking from so terrible a responsibility; and then, his heart swelling with humiliation, he turned tail and steamed sullenly away. That night there was joy in Apia; and the Germans, lately boastful, went about with shamefaced looks.

Soon afterwards, Leary set sail for Honolulu, whence he might send despatches to his Government. In his absence, the Germans tried to accomplish on land what they had failed to do on water. It was known that the Samoans had gathered in large numbers in the interior of the island, and that they were in arms against the king whom Germany had tried to force upon them. A dare-devil American named Klein, a correspondent of the New York "World," was with them, and acted as a sort of military leader. The Germans laid a plan to surprise them and to seize their chiefs. On December 18, 1888, long before daylight, a battalion of marines was disembarked from the German cruiser and marched stealthily through the forest. An hour later, the Samoans fell upon them and whirled them back to the seashore with a loss of fifty men and several officers. The fury of the Germans was unrestrained. Vice-Consul Blacklock telegraphed to Washington soon after:

"Germans swear vengeance. Shelling and burning indiscriminately, regardless of American property. Protest unheeded. Natives exasperated. Foreigners' lives and property in greatest danger. Germans respect no neutral territory. Americans in boats, fleeing. American flag seized in Apia harbor by armed German boats, but released. Admiral with squadron necessary immediately."

Up to this time, the situation in Samoa had aroused but little interest in the United States. Samoa was very far away. Most Americans had never even heard of it. But this stirring cablegram, followed as it was by detailed accounts of German aggression and of insults to the American flag, roused the people to a warlike mood. To this mood President Cleveland's Government responded. The warships "Nipsic" and "Vandalia" were hurried off to Apia, followed shortly by the "Trenton," the flagship of Admiral Kimberly, a fine old sea-dog of the fighting type. The British Government at last took heart of grace and ordered the cruiser "Calliope" to Samoa. The Germans were no less active; and early in March there were anchored off Apia, besides the vessels just enumerated, a German squadron consisting of the "Adler," the "Eber," and the "Olga," all with their decks cleared and their crews ready for immediate battle. A single rash act might provoke a mighty war.

Such was the situation when President Harrison took office on March 4th. Four days later it was rumored in Germany that the "Nipsic" had fired on the "Olga." On March 10th, a despatch from Kiel, which was supposed to have come by way of Australia, reiterated the report, and added that the American vessel had been sunk by a torpedo from the "Olga." A wave of excitement swept over the whole country. In San Francisco, great crowds filled the streets and massed themselves about the newspaper offices to await the posting of further bulletins. The

DISPUTING THE SAMOAN ISLANDS 301

tone of the press was one of intense hostility to Germany. The Government at Washington began preparing for any emergency that might arise. All the vessels of the Pacific Squadron were notified to be in readiness. The new steel cruiser, "Philadelphia," was hastily equipped for service. But the news, when it came, was very different from that for which men waited. It told of a fearful battle, not with human forces, but with the elements. A fierce typhoon had struck the Samoan Islands on March 16th, and within a few hours, six of the warships that had been anchored in the harbor of Apia were driven from their moorings. The "Eber" was dashed against a coral reef and sunk. The "Adler" was capsized. The "Olga" and the "Nipsic" were hurled upon the sand; while the "Trenton" and the "Vandalia," shattered and dismantled, settled to their gun-decks in the tremendous waves. The British ship, "Calliope," alone escaped. Her captain with high courage staked the safety of his vessel upon the chance of reaching the open sea. Crowding on every pound of steam until her boilers were almost bursting, and with her machinery red hot, the British cruiser fought her way out inch by inch against the hurricane. As she passed the American flagship, Admiral Kimberly led his sailors in three hearty cheers, which were answered by the British seamen amid the shrieking of the storm. When the typhoon subsided, it was found that few lives had been lost; and Admiral Kimberly, parading the band of the "Trenton," took temporary possession of Apia to the strains of the national anthem.

The news of this disaster dispelled all thoughts of war in Germany and in the United States. Prince Bismarck proposed a conference at Berlin to deal with the Samoan situation. He was confident that he could win by his strenuous diplomacy what he had failed to gain by bluster and a show of force. He felt perhaps that his personal presence and the greatness of his fame would overawe the untrained American commissioners, as it had invariably overawed the skilled diplomatists of Europe. He had dealt with Americans before. In 1883, a Minister of the United States at Berlin, Mr. A. S. Sargent, had displeased him by one of his despatches. Bismarck therefore ordered the officials at the Foreign Office to speak only German to Mr. Sargent whenever he called. As Mr. Sargent spoke nothing but English, he was placed in a very humiliating position, and for a whole year was obliged to transact all his official business through a secretary of legation. . . .

The conference began on April 29, 1889. The United States was represented by Mr. J. A. Kasson, Mr. William Walter Phelps and Mr. G. H. Bates, Mr. Bates having already visited Samoa and made himself familiar with the conditions there. Prince Bismarck's object was to make a treaty which should recognize the political predominance of Germany in Samoa. After he had set forth his views, the American commissioners opposed them absolutely. They insisted that the United States, Great Britain and Germany should share alike, and that the rights of each should be recognized as equal. Bismarck was a great actor. He could assume at will a tremendous indignation, and work himself into a rage which his huge bulk of body made really awe-inspiring. He now resorted to this device, and frowned portentously as he growled out sentences that seemed full of menace. The Americans were thoroughly impressed by his manner, and they cabled to Secretary Blaine, informing him that the Chancellor was very irritable. Mr. Blaine at once flashed back the terse reply: "The extent of the Chancellor's irritability is not the measure of American rights."

This message so stiffened the backbone of the American commissioners that they held to their point with unyielding pertinacity. Their British colleagues, heartened by their example, united in supporting the American position. Bismarck found that he could accomplish nothing, either by threatenings or by cajolery; and at last the man of blood and iron backed down squarely, and conceded every point. Malietoa, whom the Germans had seized and exiled, was restored as King of Samoa. A general act was signed under which the three powers established a condominium in the islands. This was the first diplomatic reverse which Bismarck had encountered in all his great career, and he had met it at the hands of the United States. . . .

THE McKINLEY TARIFF BILL

By Charles Sumner Olcott

AS Charles S. Olcott reminds us in his "Life of William McKinley," from which this account is taken, by permission of Houghton Mifflin Company, the famous McKinley Bill of 1889-90 "was the most thorough and consistent revision of the tariff, from the protective point of view, that had ever been attempted." An important feature of it was the reciprocity section, the authorship of which is attributed to James G. Blaine, then Secretary of State. The Bill provided that whenever the President should be satisfied that the government of any country was imposing unequal or excessive duties on American products introduced into that country, the United States government should have the power to retaliate in kind.

The celebrity given him by this Act of Congress paved McKinley's way to the White House, although he was not elected President until 1896, when he defeated William Jennings Bryan.

ON the 17th of December (1889) Representative McKinley presented from the Committee on Ways and Means an act "to simplify the laws in relation to the collection of the revenue." This bill was a long step in the direction of making revenue laws efficient. . . .

The new proposition established a Board of General Appraisers, to whom were to be referred all questions regarding the proper classification and appraisal of importations. It was designed to relieve the courts of the duty of deciding intricate cases, many of which hinged upon technical terms of trade and involved complicated questions of classification. Such a measure should not have aroused serious opposition yet it was not passed without a struggle and then by a strict party vote. It proved to be a wise and successful measure, and was allowed to remain on the statute books by the Congress that repealed the McKinley Tariff. . . .

. . . The purpose of the bill was clearly stated:

"It is framed in the interest of the people of the United States. It is for the better defense of American homes and American industries. While securing the needed revenue, its provisions look to the occupations of our own people, their comfort and their welfare; to the successful prosecution of industrial enterprises already started, and to the opening of new lines of production where our conditions and resources will admit. Ample revenues for the wants of the Government are provided by this bill, and every reasonable encouragement is given to productive enterprises and to the labor employed therein. The aim has been to impose duties upon such foreign products as compete with our own, whether of the soil or the shop, and to enlarge the free list wherever this can be done without injury to any American industry, or wherever an existing home industry can be helped without detriment to another industry which is equally worthy of the protecting care of the Government.

"The committee believe that, inasmuch as nearly $300,000,000 are annually required to meet the expenses of the Government, it is wiser to tax those foreign products which seek a market here in competition with our own than to tax our domestic products or the non-competing foreign products. The committee, responding as it believes to the sentiment of the country and the recommendations of the President, submit what they consider to be a just and equitable revision of the Tariff, which, while preserving that measure of protection which is required for our industrial independence, will secure a reduction of the revenue both from customs and internal revenue sources. We have not looked alone to a reduction of the revenue, but have kept steadily in view the interest of our producing classes, and have been ever mindful of that which is due to our political conditions, our labor and the character of our citizenship. We have realized that a reduction of duties below the difference between the cost of labor and production in competing countries and our own would result either in the abandonment of much of our manufacturing here or in the depression of our labor. Either result would bring disaster, the extent of which no one can measure. We have recommended no duty above the point of difference between the normal cost of production here, including labor, and the cost of like production in the countries which seek our markets, nor have we hesitated to give this measure of duty even though it involved an increase over present rates and showed an advance of percentages and 'ad-valorem' equivalents. . . . We have sought to look at the conditions of each industry at home and its relations to foreign competition, and provide for that duty which would be adequate in each case."

THE McKINLEY TARIFF BILL

The committee estimated that its recommendations, if adopted, would reduce the revenue from imports at least $60,936,536, and from internal revenue $10,327,878, an aggregate of $71,264,414. By far the greatest part of this reduction was to be obtained by remitting the duties on sugar and molasses, which in 1889 yielded $55,975,610. It was stated as a reason for this radical change that the duty on sugar was really a tax, because so large a portion of the amount consumed was necessarily imported. In this respect it differed materially from duties laid on articles produced or manufactured in the United States in sufficient quantity to meet the needs of our people. But protection was not to be denied the producers of sugar in this country and therefore a bounty of two cents a pound was to be paid on all sugars produced in the United States for fifteen years. The estimated cost of this bounty was $7,000,000. . . .

. . . The Republican Party in its platforms of 1884 and of 1888 had specifically demanded protection for the wool-growing industry. McKinley proposed a small increase of one cent a pound in the duties of wool of the first class, nothing on the second class, and an advance from five to eight cents per pound on the third class. This encouragement and defensive legislation would, in his judgment, enable the United States to produce all the wool it consumed, —about 600,000,000 pounds. . . .

There is no doubt that the section of the McKinley Bill which attracted the greatest amount of attention was the proposition to increase the duty on tin plate. . . .

It had been taken for granted for many years that tin plate could not be made in the United States. In 1873-75 attempts were made to manufacture it, but before the effort could be fairly started the foreign makers crushed the threatened competition by reducing the price from $12 a box to $4.50. When the American mills were put out of existence the price was advanced to $9 and $10 a box. From that time until 1890 the Welsh manufacturers enjoyed a monopoly and fixed their own prices. . . .

In the Committee of the Whole the duty was fixed at 2.2 cents a pound instead of one cent as provided by the Act of 1883.

. . . Thus, by the operation of a wise piece of legislation, a great industry was transferred from Wales to this country. . . .

The McKinley Bill was the most thorough and consistent revision of the Tariff, from the protective point of view, that had ever been attempted. It was, as the author declared, "protective in every paragraph and American in every line and word."

BEHRING SEA TROUBLES WITH GREAT BRITAIN

Official Communication of Secretary Blaine to British Minister Pauncefote

WAR between Great Britain and the United States over Behring Sea sealing rights was narrowly averted by the diplomatic negotiations of 1890 here recorded, which resulted in the modus vivendi between Britain and the States signed June 15, 1891. Canada was at the bottom of the trouble, Canadian sealers doing such wholesale poaching that in 1889 several Canadian vessels were seized. Thereupon Great Britain made a threat of war against the United States if such seizures continued.

Arbitration was resorted to, and what is known as the Blaine-Pauncefote Treaty provided for a tribunal which met at Paris in 1893 and framed regulations to prohibit all pelagic sealing within 60 miles of the Pribylov rookeries. The restrictions were never strictly observed, and by 1900 the Canadian sealing fleet numbered 33 vessels, with a catch of over 35,000 seals a year. In 1911 an international agreement was entered into to save the seals from extinction.

IN the opinion of the President, the Canadian vessels arrested and detained in the Behring Sea were engaged in a pursuit that was in itself "contra bonos mores," a pursuit which of necessity involves a serious and permanent injury to the rights of the Government and the people of the United States. To establish this ground it is not necessary to argue the question of the extent and nature of the sovereignty of this Government over the waters of the Behring Sea; it is not necessary to explain, certainly not to define, the powers and privileges ceded by His Imperial Majesty the Emperor of Russia in the treaty by which the Alaskan territory was transferred to the United States. The weighty considerations growing out of the acquisition of that territory, with all rights on land and sea inseparably connected therewith, may be safely left out of view, while the grounds are set forth upon which this government rests its justification for the action complained of by Her Majesty's Government.

It cannot be unknown to Her Majesty's Government that one of the most valuable sources of revenue from the Alaskan possessions is the fur-seal fisheries of the Behring Sea. Those fisheries had been exclusively controlled by the Government of Russia, without interference or without question, from their original discovery until the cession of Alaska to the United States in 1867. From 1867 to 1886 the possession in which Russia had been undisturbed was enjoyed by this Government also. There was no interruption and no intrusion from any source. Vessels from other nations passing from time to time through Behring Sea to the Arctic Ocean in pursuit of whales had always abstained from taking part in the capture of seals.

This uniform avoidance of all attempts to take furseal in those waters had been a constant recognition of the right held and exercised first by Russia and subsequently by this Government. It has also been the recognition of a fact now held beyond denial or doubt that the taking of seals in the open sea rapidly leads to their extinction. This is not only the well-known opinion of experts, both British and American, based upon prolonged observation and investigation, but the fact has also been demonstrated in a wide sense by the well-nigh total destruction of all seal fisheries except the one in the Behring Sea, which the Government of the United States is now striving to preserve, not altogether for the use of the American people, but for the use of the world at large. . . .

Whence did the ships of Canada derive the right to do in 1886 that which they had refrained from doing for more than ninety years? Upon what grounds did Her Majesty's Government defend in the year 1886 a course of conduct in the Behring Sea which she had carefully avoided ever since the discovery of that sea? By what reasoning did Her Majesty's Government conclude that an act may be committed with impunity against the rights of the United States which had never been attempted against the same rights when held by the Russian Empire? . . .

The ground upon which Her Majesty's Government justifies, or at least defends, the course of the Canadian vessels, rests upon the fact that they are committing their acts of destruction on the high seas, viz., more than three marine miles from the shore line. It is doubtful whether Her Majesty's Government would abide by this rule if the attempt were made to interfere with the pearl fisheries of Ceylon, which extend more than twenty miles from the shore line and have been enjoyed by England without molestation ever since their acquisition. So well recognized is the British ownership of those fisheries, regardless of the limit of the three-mile line that Her Majesty's Government feels authorized to sell the pearl-fishing right from year to year to the highest bidder. Nor is it credible that modes of fishing on the Grand Banks, altogether practicable but highly destructive, would be justified or even permitted by Great Britain on the plea that the vicious acts were committed more than three miles from shore.

There are, according to scientific authority, "great colonies of fish" on the "Newfoundland banks." These colonies resemble the seats of great population on land. They remain stationary, having a limited range of water in which to live and die. In these great "colonies" it is, according to expert judgment, comparatively easy to explode dynamite or giant powder in such a way as to kill vast quantities of fish, and at the same time destroy countless numbers of eggs. Stringent laws have been necessary to prevent the taking of fish by the use of dynamite in many of the rivers and lakes of the United States. The same mode of fishing could readily be adopted with effect on the more shallow parts of the banks, but the destruction of fish in proportion to the catch, says a high authority, might be as great as ten thousand to one. Would Her Majesty's Government think that so wicked an act could not be prevented and its perpetrators punished simply because it had been committed outside of the three-mile line?

Why are not the two cases parallel? . . .

In this contention the Government of the United States has no occasion and no desire to withdraw or modify the positions which it has at any time maintained against the claims of the Imperial Government of Russia. The United States will not withhold from any nation the privileges which it demanded for itself when Alaska was part of the Russian Empire.

Prime Minister Salisbury to Minister Pauncefote

It is an axiom of international maritime law that such action is only admissible in the case of piracy or in the pursuance of special international agreement. The principle has been universally admitted by jurists, and was very distinctly laid down by President Tyler in his special message to Congress, dated the 27th of February, 1843, when, after acknowledging the right to detain and search a vessel on suspicion of piracy, he goes on to say: "With this single exception, no nation has, in time of peace, any authority to detain the ships of another upon the high seas, on any pretext whatever, outside of the territorial jurisdiction."

Now, the pursuit of seals in the open sea, under whatever circumstances, has never hitherto been considered as piracy by any civilized state. Nor, even if the United States had gone so far as to make the killing of fur-seals piracy by their franchises, and privileges now belonging to Russia in the said territory or dominions and appurtenances thereto." Neither by the treaty with Russia of 1825, nor by its renewal in 1843, nor by its second renewal in 1859, did Great Britain gain any right to take seals in Behring Sea.

SECRETARY BLAINE TO MINISTER PAUNCEFOTE

Great Britain contends that the phrase "Pacific Ocean," as used in the treaties, was intended to include, and does include, the body of water which is now known as the Behring Sea. The United States contends that the Behring Sea was not mentioned, or even referred to, in either treaty, and was in no sense included in the phrase "Pacific Ocean." If Great Britain can maintain her position that the Behring Sea at the time of the treaties with Russia of 1824 and 1825 was included in the Pacific Ocean, the Government of the United States has no well-grounded complaint against her. If, on the other hand, this Government can prove beyond all doubt that the Behring Sea, at the date of the treaties, was understood by the three signatory Powers to be a separate body of water, and was not included in the phrase "Pacific Ocean," then the American case against Great Britain is great and undeniable.

The dispute prominently involves the meaning of the phrase "northwest coast," or "northwest coast of America." Lord Salisbury assumes that the "northwest coast" has but one meaning, and that it includes the whole coast stretching northward to the Behring Straits. The contention of this Government is that by long prescription the "northwest coast" means the coast of the Pacific Ocean south of the Alaska Peninsula, or south of the sixtieth parallel of north latitude; or, to define it still more accurately, the coast from the northern border of the Spanish possessions, ceded to the United States in 1819, to the point where the Spanish claims met the claims of Russia, viz., from 42° to 60° north latitude. . . . Russia practically withdrew the operation of the ukase of 1821 from the waters of the northwest coast of the Pacific Ocean, but the proof is conclusive that it was left in full force over the waters of the Behring Sea. . . . It is easy to prove from other sources that in the treaty between the United States and Russia the coast referred to was that which I have defined as the "northwest coast" of the Pacific Ocean south of 60° north latitude, or, as the Russians for a long time believed it, 59° 30'. We have in the Department of State the original of the protocols between our Minister at St. Petersburg, Mr. Henry Middleton, and Count Nesselrode, of Russia, who negotiated the treaty of 1824. . . . We feel justified in asking His Lordship if the Government of Great Britain has uniformly illustrated these precepts by example, or whether she has not established at least one notable precedent which would justify us in making greater demands upon Her Majesty's Government touching the Behring Sea than either our necessities or our desires have ever suggested. . . . Napoleon was promptly sent by Great Britain to the island of St. Helena as a prisoner for life. Six months after he reached St. Helena the British Parliament enacted a special and extraordinary law for the purpose of making his detention more secure. . . . The statute . . .

forbids them to "hover within eight leagues of the coast of the island." The penalty for hovering within eight leagues of the coast is the forfeiture of the ship to His Majesty the King of Great Britain, on trial to be had in London, and the offenses to be the same as if committed in the county of Middlesex. . . .

The repeated assertions that the Government of the United States demands that the Behring Sea be pronounced "mare clausum," are without foundation. The Government has never claimed it and never desired it. It expressly disavows it. At the same time the United States does not lack abundant authority, according to the ablest exponents of International law, for holding a small section of the Behring Sea for the protection of the fur-seals. Controlling a comparatively restricted area of water for the one specific purpose is by no means the equivalent of declaring the sea, or any part thereof, "mare clausum." Nor is it by any means so serious an obstruction as Great Britain assumed to make in the South Atlantic, nor so groundless an interference with the common law of the sea as is maintained by British authority to-day in the Indian Ocean.

Modus Vivendi between Great Britain and the United States

1. Her Majesty's Government will prohibit, until May next, seal killing in that part of Behring Sea lying eastward of the line of demarcation described in Article No. 1 of the treaty of 1867 between the United

States and Russia, "and will promptly use its best efforts to insure the observance of this prohibition by British subjects and vessels."

2. The United States Government will prohibit seal killing for the same period in the same part of Behring Sea, and on the shores and islands thereof, the property of the United States (in excess of 7,500 to be taken on the islands for the subsistence and care of the natives), and will promptly use its best efforts to insure the observance of this prohibition by United States citizens and vessels.

3. Every vessel or person offending against this prohibition in the said waters of Behring Sea outside of the ordinary territorial limits of the United States, may be seized and detained by the naval or other duly commissioned officers of either of the High Contracting Parties, but they shall be handed over as soon as practicable to the authorities of the nation to which they respectively belong, who shall alone have jurisdiction to try the offense and impose the penalties for the same. . . .

4. In order to facilitate such proper inquiries as Her Majesty's Government may desire to make, with a view to the presentation of the case of that Government before arbitrators, and in expectation that an agreement for arbitration may be arrived at, it is agreed that suitable persons designated by Great Britain will be permitted at any time, upon application, to visit or to remain upon the seal islands during the present sealing season for that purpose.